NEVER

PARENTING IN THE POWER
OF THE HOLY SPIRIT

ALONE

JEANNIE CUNNION

Lifeway Press® Nashville, Tennessee

Published by Lifeway Press® • ©2021 Jeannie Cunnion

ISBN: 978-1-0877-2905-3 • Item: 005829239

Dewey decimal classification: 231.3

Subject heading: HOLY SPIRIT / MOTHERHOOD / PARENTING

Unless otherwise noted, all Scripture quotations are from the ESV® Bible (The Holy Bible, English Standard Version®), copyright © 2001 by Crossway, a publishing ministry of Good News Publishers. Used by permission. Scripture quotations marked (AMP) are taken from the Amplified Bible, Copyright © 1954, 1958, 1962, 1964, 1965, 1987 by The Lockman Foundation. Used by permission. Scripture quotations marked NLV are taken from the New Life Version, Copyright © 1969 and 2003. Used by permission of Barbour Publishing, Inc., Uhrichsville, Ohio 44683. All rights reserved. Scripture taken from the Good News Translation in Today's English Version, Second Edition.Copyright © 1992 by American Bible Society. Used by permission. Scripture quotations marked CSB have been taken from the Christian Standard Bible®, Copyright © 2017 by Holman Bible Publishers. Used by permission. Christian Standard Bible® and CSB® are federally registered trademarks of Holman Bible Publishers. Scripture quotations marked NIV are from THE HOLY BIBLE, NEW INTERNATIONAL VERSION®, NIV® Copyright © 1973, 1978, 1984, 2011 by Biblica, Inc.® Used by permission. All rights reserved worldwide. Scripture quotations marked MSG are from The Message. Copyright © 1993, 1994, 1995, 1996, 2000, 2001, 2002. Used by permission of NavPress Publishing Group. All rights reserved. Represented by Tyndale House Publishers, Inc. Scripture quotations marked NLT are from the Holy Bible, New Living Translation, copyright © 1996, 2004, 2015 by Tyndale House Foundation. Used by permission of Tyndale House Publishers Inc., Carol Stream, Illinois 60188. All rights reserved.

To order additional copies of this resource, write Lifway Resources Customer Service; One Lifeway Plaza; Nashville, TN 37234-0113; FAX order to 615.251.5933; call toll-free 800.458.2772; email orderentry@lifeway.com; or order online at www.lifeway.com.

Printed in the United States of America

Lifeway Women Bible Studies, Lifeway Church Resources, One Lifeway Plaza, Nashville, TN 37234-0152

EDITORIAL TEAM, LIFEWAY WOMEN BIBLE STUDIES

Becky Loyd
Director, Lifeway Women

Tina Boesch
Manager, Lifeway Women Bible Studies

Sarah Doss
Publishing Team Leader, Lifeway Women Bible Studies

Lindsey Bush
Content Editor

Emily Chadwell
Production Editor

Chelsea Waack
Graphic Designer

Lauren Ervin
Cover Design

CONTENTS

ABOUT THE AUTHOR

Jeannie Cunnion is the author of *Don't Miss Out*; *Mom Set Free* book and Bible study; and *Parenting the Wholehearted Child*. As a self-described grace-clinger, Jeannie's writing is woven with wisdom, humility, humor, and a contagious love for the good news. She is also a beloved Bible teacher and frequent speaker at women's conferences and parenting events around the country.

Jeannie holds a master's degree in social work, and her writing has been featured on outlets such as *The Today Show*, *Fox News*, *The 700 Club*, *LIFE Today*, and *Focus on the Family*.

Jeannie and her husband, Mike, are the proud parents of five boys who range from five to twenty-four. Her hobbies include grocery shopping—because, five boys—and praying—because again, five boys. When not cheering for her boys on the sidelines, you'll most likely find her singing worship music off-key in her kitchen while trying not to burn dinner again. To know Jeannie is to know her deep love for Danita's Children's Home in Haiti.

She would love to connect with you on Instagram @JeannieCunnion and on her website at jeanniecunnion.com.

INTRODUCTION

Of *all* the things I thought God would lead me to write about in my next Bible study, the power of the Holy Spirit wasn't one of them. I didn't see this one coming.

Maybe you can relate? Of all the Bible studies you thought you'd explore about parenting, you didn't expect to study how the presence and power of the Holy Spirit can make such a radical difference in how you lead and love your kids. Or maybe this is exactly what you've been waiting for and knew you needed!

Wherever you land, I'm just so grateful you're holding this study in your hands, because the Holy Spirit plays an absolutely vital role in our ability to be the moms we long to be. To be totally transparent, this isn't a truth I understood or appreciated until I began to study the full scope of the Holy Spirit's work in our lives. It was only in following the Lord's leading to write this study that I began to be blown away by what I discovered and encountered in the beautiful but often neglected person of the Holy Spirit. All of that to say, I offer this study to you with great humility, praying that it will help you grow in your knowledge of and personal relationship with the Spirit.

THE BACKSTORY

My desire to have a deeper understanding of the Holy Spirit's power began about a year after my last Bible study, *Mom Set Free*, was released. *Mom Set Free* is about embracing and enjoying the freedom for which Christ has set us free as women and as moms. But while I was busy speaking at conferences about our freedom in Christ, I began to struggle again at home with patterns and fears from which I'd been set free. Yes, we are indeed forgetful people who never outgrow our need to hear the hope of the gospel every day.

Around this same time, I was invited to speak to a lovely group of moms about relying on the Holy Spirit to accomplish His work in our kids' lives. When I finished speaking, we opened up the discussion for Q&A, and that was when one wise woman asked a significant question: "I know we are supposed to rely on the Holy Spirit, but how do we actually do that? How do we access His power and teach it to our kids?" The truth is, I didn't have a very helpful answer for her, beyond explaining how Scripture tells us to ask for His help and trust He will show up.

That's when I began to grapple with the question, *Do I really know how to parent in the power of the Holy Spirit, or have I settled for parenting in my own power?*

After months of reflection and paying attention to patterns in my parenting, I knew the honest answer was I've mostly settled for my own power. I wasn't fully dependent on the Holy Spirit's help. This revelation led me to a passionate pursuit of understanding who the Holy Spirit is, what the Holy Spirit does, and how I could become a more Spirit-empowered mom.

What I discovered as I searched the Scriptures is what propelled me to write this study: I was set free by Jesus, but I was still trying to live free by Jeannie.

I was still trying to parent in my natural power rather than in the Spirit's super-natural power. I was still trying to play the Holy Spirit's role in my kids' lives. I was still trying to meet the demands of motherhood without the help of the Helper. And, boy, was I ever settling for less than what God wanted to do in me, produce through me, and put on display for my kids to see.

I want you to know I am not attempting to answer all of our questions about the Holy Spirit in this study. The Holy Spirit is as mysterious as He is made-known, and questions will remain around the more complex and controversial conversations we could (but won't) have about the Holy Spirit. This is not an extensive theological treatise about the Holy Spirit but a personal invitation to better know and enjoy Him.

This sparked a deep desire to personally know and encounter all of God—God the Father, God the Son, and God the Holy Spirit.

Mamas, we need help! God designed us to need Him and then He gave us the help of the Holy Spirit to fill our need! He gave us holy help, a help beyond our comprehension!

We are *never alone* to navigate any of the challenges or trials or hardships we encounter in our parenting. I think it's fair to say we often carry huge backpacks filled with heavy burdens. But the Spirit of God wants to lighten our loads by taking those burdens we were never meant to carry and laying them before the Father on our behalf. He wants to champion us!

He wants to …

- show us His power when the pressures of parenting feel crushing;
- take us by the hand and guide us as we guide our children;
- put truth on our tongues to share with our struggling teens;

- bring hope into our hurting hearts for our prodigal daughters and sons;
- infuse us with strength when the endless tasks of raising toddlers are overwhelming us;
- increase our capacity when we say, "It's too much. I can't do this another day";
- bring peace to our chaotic minds;
- fill us with joy in what typically feels like mundane deeds;
- cultivate deeper intimacy in our relationship with Jesus;
- comfort us in our loneliness or sadness;
- counsel us as we make choices on behalf of our children;
- absolutely assure us that His presence in us is greater than anything we will encounter;
- fill us with God's love and produce God-glorifying fruit in our lives for our children to witness.

This is what He delights to do! The question is, will we let Him?

I wasn't fully letting Him. But here's the thing, neglecting the Holy Spirit wasn't an intentional decision. I simply didn't know very much about why His specific work in my life mattered so much. I think that's how it is for a lot of us. We just don't know.

I've been following Jesus since I was eight years old. I know and believe the core doctrines of Christianity, among them that the Holy Spirit is an equal and essential member of the Trinity. I wholeheartedly recite the creeds. I sing worship songs about the Spirit's power, and I had plenty of exposure to His work as a preacher's kid in a charismatic church. But I didn't know all of the benefits I was missing out on by not being more aware of and reliant on the Spirit's presence and power in my life. I undervalued His personhood, and I underestimated His power.

But God, in His infinite kindness, heard my daily prayers for a fuller knowledge and experience of His love in Jesus, and He answered those prayers by reintroducing me to His Spirit.

AN INVITATION TO ENJOY THE HOLY SPIRIT
I believe the Holy Spirit is about to blow us away with the difference He can make in the high calling of motherhood. I can say that to you with such confidence because through the writing of this study, I have begun to cherish how the Holy Spirit brings intimacy in my relationship with Jesus. I have become expectant for how His supernatural power will continue to strengthen my heart and manifest in

my mothering. I've come to discover how much better life is when I stay in step with the Spirit, what a better mother I am when I'm not trying to do it without Him, and what a disaster I am when I don't take the help! And I'm confident this is what will unfold in your life too, if you come open to receive all that He wants to do in you and for you.

If we invite the Holy Spirit to do business with us and are willing to open our hearts to the places where He wants to grow us in obedience and trust, we can confidently know that He will give us the grace to receive it. He speaks into our broken places and our battle with the flesh with grace.

This is the best news! *All* of God is accessible to us, and this will be our aim. He's not withholding His Spirit from us. On the contrary, He's eagerly waiting for us to welcome His activity in our lives—activity that will radically change how we walk alongside our children under the sovereignty of God.

Also, before we dive in, I'd be remiss if I didn't mention this: If you haven't put your trust in Jesus, and you don't have the Holy Spirit's indwelling presence, please keep reading, as this study is every bit as much for you! The very fact that you're reading this tells me God is in passionate pursuit of you, patiently waiting for you to say yes to Jesus and receive His Spirit.

Or maybe your faith life feels dull and tired, and you've wondered what you're missing. Or maybe you've simply been longing to go deeper in your faith. I hope you'll see this study as an invitation to know how the Holy Spirit brings vibrancy to and greater intimacy in your relationship with Jesus.

Or maybe you already enjoy the Holy Spirit as a close companion, but you're eager to discover more about how to parent in His power.

Wherever you land, I am so glad you are holding this study in your hand. Sister, I am so expectant imagining how our relationships with Jesus will flourish in the wake of our awakening to the Holy Spirit, and how His love will fill our hearts, overflow into our homes, and impact how our children walk in the knowledge and power of the Three-in-One, the eternal triune God.

So let's ask God to manifest His Spirit in our lives and in our parenting in a fresh way, with the ultimate goal being hearts enlarged for Jesus. That is the Holy Spirit's ministry and mission after all—to make much of Jesus!

Jeannie

#NeverAloneBibleStudy

THE PRESENCE OF THE HOLY SPIRIT

When our son Cal was about to turn thirteen, I asked a group of men in his life to write him a letter addressing what attributes they saw in Cal and what wisdom they wanted to impart to him. I assembled the letters in a journal we gave him on his birthday. The group included relatives, longtime family friends, coaches, church leaders, and men in our community who do life closely alongside us and know Cal well.

The letters were beyond anything I could have expected. I read them through tears of gratitude for the thoughtfulness they held. What an extraordinary gift we got to give our son. Because we found this gift to be so powerful in Cal's life, we decided to continue the tradition with all of our boys. So when our son Brennan recently turned thirteen, we gave him a journal filled with letters as well. Again, I was blown away by the beauty and thoughtfulness of them. But there is one letter in particular I want to share with you, because really, it's for all of us. It was written by our friend Blaze. He and his wife, Desi, lead a church in our area, and they have become cherished family friends. After Blaze described the unique strengths he sees in Brennan, he wrote:

Your job, as you grow into a man, is to learn how to steward the gifts the Holy Spirit has given you and to grow in the anointing that is on your life. I wish I could give you the road map on how to do that but that would defeat God's purpose, which is for you to go to Him. But I can promise you this—your life will be infinitely greater than you could ever imagine if you stay close to God. The gifts the Holy Spirit has given you will take you far without Him—but with Him—you will go places you could have never dreamed of! He will do more with you, through you, and around you than you thought possible. Trust me on this!

Blaze's letter to Brennan reminded me that one of the primary roles in my life as a mom is to learn how to steward the gifts the Holy Spirit has given me and to grow in the anointing that is on my life. In doing so, the Holy Spirit is invited to do more with me, through me, and around me than I ever thought possible. This is true for each one of us.

DAY 1
HE IS FOR OUR GOOD

To begin, I think it will be helpful for us to ensure we have a solid understanding of the relationship between God the Father, God the Son, and God the Holy Spirit, although we'll look at this much more closely in Session 2. For now, however, let's acknowledge together how the Holy Spirit unites us to the Son, Jesus Christ, to receive the life and love of the Father. The Spirit isn't an added feature of our salvation; He is the power and comfort we receive through our faith in Christ.

Put another way (and using some "begets" and "begottens" that may be uncommon to us but show up a lot in descriptions of the Trinity): the Triune persons are only differentiated by the eternal relations of origin. The Father eternally begets the Son. The Son is eternally begotten of the Father. The Spirit eternally proceeds from the Father and the Son. Then, when God acts in salvation history, the Father sends the Son. The Son is sent by the Father, and the Spirit is sent by the Father and the Son.

Now please draw a diagram of what I just described. Just kidding! But it's helpful to have this foundation to build on. OK, let's talk about how this is for our good.

Mamas, when we put our trust in Jesus, we become connected to the Godhead! As I mentioned in the Introduction, we become anointed by the Holy Spirit. Let's make sure we grasp the magnitude of this.

> Read the following passages, making a note about what you learn from each:
>
> John 14:16-17
>
> John 16:7
>
> Romans 8:11
>
> Titus 3:5

In the Old Testament, people or things were anointed as a sign and symbol of their being set apart by God for a specific purpose or task. The Old Testament leaves us with an anticipation of a different kind of anointing that would come with the Holy

Spirit. We see an example of this when the prophet Samuel took oil and anointed a young shepherd boy named David. As David was anointed, the Holy Spirit "rushed upon" him from that day forward (1 Sam. 16:13).

In the New Testament, however, the Holy Spirit anointed Christians in a full, complete, and definitive manner (Acts 10:38; 1 John 2:20,27). When we are anointed by the Holy Spirit we are set apart as holy to reflect the holiness of the Father in Christ illuminated in our lives by the power of the Spirit. As a byproduct for us as parents, we gain the Spirit's wisdom and strength to help us lead and love the children He has entrusted to us.

Do we appreciate the immeasurable benefits of this anointing? The truth is, I didn't. I didn't know what I was missing out on by not having a deeper knowledge of and relationship with the Holy Spirit. I didn't realize how much I was living in my own strength and supply by not being more dependent on the Spirit.

My posture with the Spirit of God was one more of hesitation than coop-eration, and not because I didn't affirm the triune God—Father, Son, and Holy Spirit. I wholeheartedly did. My neglect of the Holy Spirit was primarily because I didn't understand His distinct and essential role in a flourishing faith. The result? I had all of Him, but He didn't have all of me.

Another obstacle to many of us enjoying the Holy Spirit is the many misconceptions about Him. I believe Satan has made it his mission to malign the reputation of the Holy Spirit, and sadly, he's been pretty successful. He has kept too many Christians tiptoeing in the shallow end of the Living Water, barely experiencing the refreshment offered us in the Spirit, because we're afraid of what we've seen done in His name.

Where does your relationship with the Holy Spirit land on this spectrum?

Hesitation ▬▬▬▬▬▬▬▬▬▬▬▬▬ Cooperation

Fear ▬▬▬▬▬▬▬▬▬▬▬▬▬▬ Trust

Skeptical ▬▬▬▬▬▬▬▬▬▬▬▬ Curious

Dismissive ▬▬▬▬▬▬▬▬▬▬▬ Welcoming

"The eternal triune God reveals Himself to us as Father, Son, and Holy Spirit with distinct personal attributes, but without division of nature, essence or being."[1]

What experiences have formed your opinion of or attitude toward the Holy Spirit? This is really important. Take some time to reflect and write.

If you're someone who has a deeply personal and trusting friendship with the Holy Spirit, recognize this is a precious and even rare gift, because I've had enough conversations with Christian women to know that many of us are comfortable with God the Father and God the Son, but we assume God the Spirit is reserved for the extremes: either the super-spiritual or the super-strange.

If we wouldn't ascribe to either of these extremes, we might assume His benefits are for other Christians but not for us. So we happily recite the seven words we often find in Scripture—"through the power of the Holy Spirit"—but rarely do we actually know how to live in His transforming power, or if we even want to. And we almost certainly don't consistently experience that power infusing our parenting.

TO OUR ADVANTAGE
Read John 16:5-7.

Depending on the translation of your Bible, you may have read how Jesus said it is "for your good" (NIV) or "to your advantage" (ESV) or "for your benefit" (CSB) that He returns to the Father.

In this passage Jesus prepared His disciples for His ascension and the forthcoming ministry of the Holy Spirit. This was by no means the first time Jesus spoke to His disciples about sending the Holy Spirit to be their (and our) Helper, but Jesus' departure at this point was imminent. He provided a final word of comfort and encouragement to His grieving disciples about the significance of the Holy Spirit's coming.

Why did Jesus say it was for our good? Refer to the end of verse 7 and write the reason below.

The Helper (the Advocate) is, of course, the Holy Spirit. But the disciples couldn't fathom how Jesus could say such a thing. *How could it ever be to our advantage or for our good that You go away and "only" leave us with Your Spirit?*

This wasn't just disappointing news to the disciples. It was devastating. They'd spent three years by His side and under His leadership, and this wasn't how they expected it to go down. They felt like Jesus was abandoning them when He was supposed to be setting up His kingdom among them!

> Has your posture toward the Holy Spirit been similar to or different from how the disciples responded? Why?

My response has been much like the disciples' response. "But Jesus, I want *You*."

What the disciples didn't understand is that when Jesus returned to the Father, they would lose physical closeness with Jesus but gain something far more valuable: deeper connectivity to Jesus because God's Spirit would take up residence within them. They would each become the new temple in whom the Spirit would reside:

> *Do you not know that you are God's temple*
> *and that God's Spirit dwells in you?*
> **1 CORINTHIANS 3:16**

You see, Jesus was "God with us." The Holy Spirit is "God in us." Jesus wasn't giving them less of Him; He was giving them even more.

OUR NEW BIRTHRIGHT
OPEN YOUR BIBLE and read Romans 8:9-11.

> What did the Spirit of God do? (Refer to v. 11.) Where does this same Spirit of God live now? (Refer to the end of v. 11.)

In this teaching on the life-giving Spirit, Paul emphasized that if you have put your trust in Christ, you belong to God and have the Holy Spirit dwelling in you. A Spirit-filled life is your new birthright in Christ. This is why the Holy Spirit's presence is for our good! From His virgin conception, God the Son, Jesus Christ, experienced life as both human and divine. He came so He could identify with every trial and temptation that comes at us. And He came so He could pay the price for the sins that enslave us.

But now, because of Jesus' glorification, the disciples would never be without God's presence and power in the Person of the Holy Spirit. The Spirit represents the love between God the Father and God the Son (Rom. 5:5; Eph. 4). Everything God would call the disciples to do would be fueled by the power of God inside them.

And that is just as true for us today as it was for the disciples more than two thousand years ago. We are never without everything we need when we have the Holy Spirit, and this extends to our parenting. Everything God has commissioned you to do as a parent is meant to be carried out in the resurrection power of His Spirit.

The Holy Spirit's power is absolutely essential to our ability to parent our children with God's transforming love. The Holy Spirit opens our hearts to Jesus and makes Jesus ever more beautiful to us. He matures us in the character of Christ through the growing pains of parenthood. He frees us from trying to play the role of our child's savior.

What else does the Holy Spirit do? He guides us, comforts us, counsels us, fills us with hope and joy, gives us life and peace, strengthens us in our inner being, communicates through us, prays for us, leads us in truth, empowers us to fight sin, illuminates Scripture, and advocates for us before the Father. He gives us supernatural gifts to build up the church and glorify God in our homes. He reminds us that absolutely nothing in all this world is better than Jesus. He glorifies Christ. This, and still more, is what we'll discover in the weeks ahead.

> What surprises you most about the scope of the Holy Spirit's work in the paragraphs you just read? Explain.

> What do you expect will be of most benefit in this season of parenting? Explain.

I'm so excited about what God is going to do in, through, and around us as we grow in deeper knowledge, dependence, and love of His Spirit.

DAY 2
HE MAKES HIS HOME IN US

You know how it feels when you're falling in love? You can't get enough of that person. You become completely preoccupied with them and want to spend as much time as you can in their presence. That can be true when you're falling in love in the early stage of a relationship, but it can be equally as true in seasons when you fall in love all over again with your spouse. I remember my preoccupation with my husband, Mike, when we started dating. We were set up by my childhood best friend, Morella. Oh yes, she was unashamed in her scheme to introduce me to one of her husband's best friends. Obviously her plan was successful because Mike has been my favorite human basically since the day I laid eyes on him. And the more I discovered about him, the more I wanted to know of him. Here is why I'm sharing this story with you: getting to know the Holy Spirit has felt a lot like those early days with Mike. The more I've gotten to know the Holy Spirit, the more I've wanted to know of Him. The more I've opened myself up to Him, the more trustworthy I've found Him to be. The Holy Spirit is so lovable. And likable.

The key difference is that, unlike the newness of my relationship with Mike when we were first dating, I'm not discovering the Holy Spirit for the first time. He's been with me all along. Actually, He hasn't just been with me. He's been dwelling in my heart since the day Jesus became my King. So it's been more like a rediscovery of the Holy Spirit. God has been reintroducing me to His Spirit and showing me how His indwelling presence allows me to enjoy the fullness of the Trinity. The more I've discovered about the Holy Spirit, who is the priceless treasure placed inside our hearts, the more I've desired to understand how He enables us to live a free and full life infused with God's power.

OPEN YOUR BIBLE and read John 14:15-17.

We will return to this passage many times throughout our study because there is so much truth to discover. But first let's unpack two points.

1. ANOTHER HELPER

Fill in the blanks based on verse 16:

"And I will ask the Father, and he _____
_____."

The Greek word translated "helper" in this verse is *paraklētos*, literally meaning "called to one's side."[2] But this wasn't just any helper. Even more exciting is how Jesus said the Holy Spirit would be "another Helper." The Greek word translated "another" in this verse is *allon*— which, in this context, translates "another of the same kind."[3] So Jesus assured the disciples that the Holy Spirit isn't "less than" Him or even "similar" to Him, but just like Him!

The Holy Spirit is the power and presence of Christ. He shares the same essence as Jesus, and yet He is His own divine Person who serves a distinct purpose in a believer's life. He continues what Jesus started. More on that later, but meanwhile, let's stay focused on this word *paraklētos*.

Divine Person means we see His divinity in the characteristics of Deity ascribed to Him. He is eternal, omnipotent, omnipresent, and omniscient. (We'll dive into this more in Session 2.)

Fill in the blanks based on what you read in the above paragraph:

The Holy Spirit is the _____ and _____ of Christ, but He is His own divine _____ who serves a distinct _____.

The Holy Spirit is the Spirit of Christ, so where the Spirit is, Jesus is.

In the ESV translation of John 14:16, the Holy Spirit is called "another Helper" by Jesus, but in the Amplified Bible—because *paraklētos* is too full of meaning to translate into just one word—the Holy Spirit is also called our "Comforter, Advocate, Intercessor—Counselor, Strengthener, Standby."

Briefly describe each of these roles the Holy Spirit plays. Use a dictionary to look up the meaning if you'd like, or just describe these roles in your own words.

A Comforter:

An Advocate:

An Intercessor:

A Counselor:

A Strengthener:

A Standby:

In your current season of parenting, which one these titles of God the Spirit brings the most relief and encouragement to you? Why?

2. INDWELLING GOD

The second thing I want us to notice from John 14:15-17 is from verse 17, when Jesus said, "You know him, for he dwells with you and will be in you."

What two ways did John say the Spirit would commune with the disciples?

The Holy Spirit isn't just beside you for companionship when you feel hopeless and overwhelmed. He isn't just in front of you to guide you as you lead your children, and He isn't just behind you to spur you on when you grow weary and want to give up.

God has put His Spirit *inside* you.

Let's do a quick glance back in history to see the significance of this. Read each verse below and then draw a line to match the verse with the corresponding preposition that defines the Holy Spirit's relationship to people at that time.

Judges 14:19   IN

John 14:17   UPON

1 Corinthians 6:19   WITH

"The operations of the Holy Spirit among humanity throughout human history may be defined by three words: 'upon,' 'with,' and 'in.' In the Old Testament the Holy Spirit came upon selected persons and remained for a season (Judg. 14:19). In the Gospels He is represented as dwelling with the disciples in the person of Christ (John 14:17). From the second chapter of Acts onward He is spoken of as being in the people of God (1 Cor. 6:19)."[4]

Living in the people of God, as Jesus told the disciples He would do, was an entirely new phenomenon because, prior to Pentecost, the Holy Spirit primarily resided upon people or with people.

Jesus referred to the words of John just before His ascension, affirming to the disciples that they would soon ("not many days from now") receive this baptism (Acts 1:5). The promise was then fulfilled on the Day of Pentecost, when the Holy Spirit came upon the 120 disciples in the upper room (Acts 2:4) and tongues of fire rested on each of them (Acts 2:3). To demonstrate publicly that He had given the Spirit, God miraculously enabled the 120 to speak in the foreign languages of the pilgrims present in Jerusalem that day (Acts 2:4-12).

Now Jesus was promising something so much greater. He said that though the disciples already knew the Holy Spirit because He was with them, now He would live *in* them. And the Spirit's indwelling presence would not be earned through each disciple's moral behavior, right theology, or good works. It would be God's gift of grace bringing about radical change within their lives (Acts 2:38; 5:32; 1 Cor. 6:19).

Jesus knew the Holy Spirit would indwell ordinary people to transform them with His extraordinary power.

> **OPEN YOUR BIBLE** and read Galatians 3:13-14.
>
> Based on this passage, how do we receive the promised Holy Spirit through faith?

Faith in Jesus is the only prerequisite to receiving God's Spirit. When we put our faith in Christ, God's Spirit abides within us. The Holy Spirit is freely given to those who repent and believe in Jesus.

After the Spirit indwelt the disciples at Pentecost, they began to preach with boldness in the power of the Holy Spirit. We'll get to Pentecost soon enough, but first I want us to read a passage that's foundational to our study.

> **OPEN YOUR BIBLE** and read Acts 2:38-39.

Peter didn't say "might"; He said "will." Peter didn't say we will "earn" the gift; he said we will "receive" it. The Holy Spirit is a free gift for all who believe.

Here's the thing: Every believer is given the gift of the Holy Spirit, but not every believer enjoys the gift.

Imagine this with me. On Christmas morning you find a wrapped gift under the tree with a tag on it. What are your choices? (1) You can read the tag, see it's for you, unwrap the gift and enjoy it entirely. (2) You can tear the paper and take a peek but leave it wrapped because it's not what you expected or hoped for. (3) You can leave the package under the tree untouched because you didn't read the tag and nobody told you it was for you.

> What have you done with the gift of the Holy Spirit? Has it looked more like the first, second, or third option?

When you believe in the finished work of Christ—His life, death, and resurrection—on your behalf, the Holy Spirit takes up residence in your spirit. The Spirit's indwelling presence unites you to the Son, so that in Him, you receive the life and love of the Father. There is absolutely nothing ordinary or insignificant about you, because as a Christian, you are home to the Holy Spirit. He lives in your inner being and works on your behalf.

I'm pretty sure we too often neglect to notice all He does and wants to do in our hearts and in our homes, and I don't want us to miss it anymore!

> Write a prayer of gratitude to God for choosing to take up residence inside you and for making all that is His, yours.

HOW DOES THIS EMPOWER MY PARENTING?

What difference does this make to us as mothers? A lot! See, I think most of us struggle with feeling insignificant and ordinary because culture is quick to devalue the hard and holy work of motherhood. So we load up our plates to prove we are capable of doing more than "just" raising small humans to be kind, courageous God-fearing adults, and we feel guilty saying, "This is already a lot! I can barely do this well."

But we as Christians know better, right? Or maybe we don't. Maybe we've felt the pressure to prove our value outside of being valued by God. Maybe we've lost sight of the truth that our highest calling is loving Jesus and making His love known. And yes, that work of making His love known begins inside our homes, but let's not miss this: Before God's love can be made known in our homes, it has to be made real in our hearts.

> When have you struggled with believing the work you do as a mother matters? Maybe you know the "big things" matter, but have you felt unseen in the daily routine of cleaning the dirty dishes, driving the carpools, and disciplining the disobedience?

> What comfort or confidence do you gain in knowing you are the home of God's Spirit in that work? Is your countenance lifted knowing your worth isn't defined by that work? Why or why not?

I can't think of anything more meaningful God could have done to prove how precious and extraordinary you are to Him than for His very Spirit to take up residence inside of you. You are indwelt by God, Mama. Your value is in knowing how valuable you are to Him, proven by His Son's death on the cross and His Spirit freely placed in Your heart. You are home to the Holy Spirit!

DAY 3
HE NEVER LEAVES US

There are few things that sting more than rejection. We've all experienced it in its various forms. Maybe you've been rejected by a parent, someone you dated, or a close friend. Maybe you've been rejected after a dream job interview or by a group you desperately wanted to fit into. Maybe you're reading this as a mama whose child has launched and he or she has since broken relationship with you or denied the faith you worked tirelessly to impart. Maybe you've experienced rejection from your spouse.

None of us is immune to rejection.

For many years I worked as an adoption counselor. It was one of the greatest privileges of my life—being able to walk alongside women experiencing unplanned pregnancies as they made plans of permanency for their child and also supporting hopeful parents-to-be as their dreams of having a child became a reality.

Though adoption is biblical and beautiful, I'm not pretending it's all rainbows and Skittles®. The process is often painful and certainly far from perfect. I recall one particular birth mom considering adoption who had actually been placed for adoption herself when she was a baby. She was struggling with her decision because she said that no matter how wanted she was by the loving parents who adopted her, and no matter how many times she was told how much her birth parents loved her, she always carried a deep-seated sense of rejection because she was placed for adoption.

Fast-forward several years later when God completely redeemed her story, reunited her with her birth parents, and revealed to her how deeply wanted and loved she truly was. She finally saw God's hand of grace on her life every single step of the way and came to the place where she could honestly say she wouldn't have changed a thing. Nothing is wasted with God.

But more than fearing rejection from people, I think a lot of us fear rejection from our heavenly Father. I remember the painful nights I put the kids to bed and then curled up on the couch and recited all of the things I wished I'd done differently and all of ways my Father must have been disappointed in me. I feared God would give up on me because I'd all but given up on ever attaining a perfection I actually thought was possible in those early years.

When have you feared rejection and abandonment by God?

What circumstances or behaviors brought that fear? Is this something you still fear now? Explain.

Do you know someone else who feared being abandoned by God? David, and for good reason.

THE PROMISE OF HIS PRESENCE

OPEN YOUR BIBLE and read 1 Samuel 10:9-11.

Fill in the blank:

When Samuel anointed Saul as the first king of Israel, verse 10 says, "The Spirit of God _____ him, and he prophesied among them."

Later, however, in 1 Samuel 16:14, God removed the presence and power of the Holy Spirit from Saul when he disobeyed God. Without the power of the Spirit, Saul couldn't successfully serve as king, and he ultimately died in battle. After God removed His Spirit from Saul, God chose David as the second king of Israel.

Read 1 Samuel 16:13.

Fill in the blank:

When Samuel took the horn of oil and anointed David in the presence of his brothers, verse 13 says, "the Spirit of the LORD _____ David."

In both anointings we see the word "upon," and that matters greatly.

David, who was often called the ideal king, has a remarkable story. From slaying Goliath to taking the ark of the covenant into Jerusalem, David served God faithfully in the power of Spirit, but like us, David was terribly human, and therefore, inherently fallible. Two such examples of his humanity are his adultery with Bathsheba and his orchestration of her husband's murder.

After the prophet Nathan confronted him, David penned Psalm 51.

OPEN YOUR BIBLE and read David's prayer in Psalm 51.

What did David beg God not to do? (See vv. 10-12.)

As we began to discuss in Day 2, in the Old Testament the Holy Spirit came upon people to equip and empower them for a specific purpose, but they couldn't count on His presence as permanent. This means God could've taken the Holy Spirit from David like He did from Saul, but He didn't. He was merciful in David's humble confession and repentance and let His Spirit remain. Allowing the Holy Spirit to remain on David didn't mean God protected him from the very painful consequences of his sin.

Like David, we will often suffer the consequences of our sin in human relationships, but unlike David, we never have to fear the ultimate consequence of losing the permanent presence of the Holy Spirit.

The profound difference between God's people in the Old Testament and us now is that we have the precious post-Pentecost promise we receive as believers. We never have to fear abandonment by the Holy Spirit. We never have to fear God will take His Spirit from us. He is with us—and in our hearts—forever.

In Day 2 we read John 14:15-17 and highlighted two takeaways from that passage. Today, let's continue to verse 18.

OPEN YOUR BIBLE and reread John 14:15-17, and this time read through verse 18.

In verse 16, Jesus said the Holy Spirit will be with us _____.

In verse 18, Jesus said He will not leave us as _____.

The Holy Spirit is the most faithful companion you and I will ever have. Quite literally, because of Jesus' promises, He is incapable of ever leaving us alone.

Growing up, I knew so little about the Holy Spirit's companionship. I knew Him mostly as a Convictor (a great gift we will unpack later), but I didn't think of Him as my Companion or my Comforter. I didn't know Him as my best friend.

However, this is the beautiful truth about the Spirit of God: His companionship isn't confined to our awareness of His presence. He stays when we pay Him no attention. He doesn't pout and walk out when we neglect Him. He remains even when we try to push Him away. We can forfeit the benefits of the anointing on our lives, but we can't force Him to give up on us.

OPEN YOUR BIBLE and read Psalm 139:7-10.

What does this passage tell you about the Holy Spirit's presence? Does that bring you comfort or make you uncomfortable? Why?

How does knowing the Spirit is always with you encourage you in your parenting today?

I might not know what valleys you're walking through currently or what you've come through, but I do know there are no circumstances that can cause the Holy Spirit to leave you behind. He doesn't give up on you when you give up on yourself. The Holy Spirit doesn't abandon you when you stumble into sin. Your sadness doesn't scare Him away. His abiding presence is internal and eternal. He is the faithful friend you long for, taking your hand and leading you toward your hope of wholeness. He is the loyal companion who comforts you in your grief and distress. And He is nearer than your own breath in the midst of your fears and loneliness.

HOW DOES THIS EMPOWER MY PARENTING?

Something we don't hear much about is how lonely motherhood can be. It may even seem silly to say moms get lonely because, in many respects, we are never alone! Right? In fact, we'll do almost anything to get some alone time. We'll hide in the bathroom or sit in our car long after we've pulled into the driveway just for a little solitude. But the truth is, motherhood can be terribly lonely, even when we're surrounded by children.

You might feel lonely because ...

- You don't have the energy to invest in friendships because you have given everything you've got to your kids and there aren't any leftovers for girlfriends.

- You are single or divorced and literally doing it alone.

- You are disconnected from your spouse—a result of exhaustion, disagreeing about how to parent your children, or from any attempt at intimacy being interrupted by little ones who will do anything to delay saying goodnight.

- You don't have friends you can trust to talk about the hardships in your home. When the kids are little, we're afraid to be honest about how overwhelming parenting littles is because we think it makes us look like incompetent moms, or even bad moms. When our littles turn into teens, we're afraid to be honest about the struggles our kids are having or the choices they're making because we're afraid it makes them look like incompetent kids, or even bad kids.

- It looks like life is passing you by. While you change diapers, try to help with math homework that now feels above your pay grade, or cart children from activity to activity, you might feel like everyone else is making their dreams come true while you're just trying to decide what to make for dinner.

The majority of what we do as mothers is done in isolation, and so much of what we do feels invisible. Because while we're making sure everyone else is OK, it feels like there's nobody under our roof making sure we are OK.

You can know you are deeply loved but still feel terribly lonely.

Which of the statements about loneliness resonates most with you?

What other factors contribute to your loneliness?

What have you done in times of loneliness to feel less alone?
Was that helpful?

What I want you to know is that you are not alone in your loneliness. Did you know that loneliness is being called the new epidemic in America? Mamas aren't the exception to this research. Sometimes there's power in just knowing we're not the only ones who feel that way.

More importantly, the beautiful benefit of having the Holy Spirit is that we really are never alone. The One who remains with us doesn't need anything from us. His goal is to draw us deeper into intimacy with Jesus—and as a result, God gives us everything we need to parent the children He has entrusted to us. Imagine the Spirit not just taking up residence inside you but also feeling His companionship beside you and His power upon you!

Close today by reading Psalm 46. Go back and note the breathtaking truth in verse 5 and then write it below.

Sister, just as God was within His city and would not let it be destroyed, God is within you by His Spirit and He will not leave you or let you fall.

DAY 4

HE MAKES MUCH OF JESUS

If you asked me what some of my favorite things about the Holy Spirit are, what we are studying today would be one of the first—if not the first—things I'd name.

OPEN YOUR BIBLE and read the words of Jesus in John 16:13-15.

In this passage, Jesus was preparing His disciples for His ascension and teaching them about the coming work of the Holy Spirit.

What are some of the things that jump out at you?

Now look specifically at verse 14. Who did Jesus say the Holy Spirit would glorify?

The word "glorify" is the Greek word *doxazō*, which can be translated a variety of ways depending on its context. It can be rendered "to praise, extol, magnify, celebrate" or "to render (or esteem) glorious."[5] In John 16:14, *doxazō* actually encompasses the full range of these meanings.

Jesus was teaching that the Holy Spirit's whole goal is to glorify Him. In everything the Holy Spirit does, He wants Jesus to be the One whom we make much of.

When Jesus said, "He will guide you into all truth" (v. 13), He was telling the disciples that the Holy Spirit would help them recall and retell the truth about who Jesus is and what Jesus accomplished. And we are the vessels through which He does this today for our children. How incredible is that?

Can I confess something to you? I didn't appreciate the significance of this until I began to study the Spirit in depth. This central role of the Holy Spirit is one of the most overlooked benefits, but this shouldn't surprise us, because we have a very real enemy who does not want us discovering the matchless love of Jesus. And He doesn't want our lives making much of Jesus with our kids.

The enemy's highest priority is to keep us from receiving salvation through Christ. There is nothing the "roaring lion" (1 Pet. 5:8) wants more than to keep you and me from inheriting the eternal blessings we receive in Christ. But, oh, once he loses that battle, he does not quit. He doubles down.

THE SCHEMES OF THE ENEMY

Once we are new creations in Christ, I believe the enemy's highest priority becomes ensuring we don't experience the freedom and fullness of God through the power of the Holy Spirit in this life (John 10:10).

He schemes by attaching stigmas to the Spirit that make us skeptical about what the Holy Spirit will do in us if we give Him full access.

> **What lies** have made us keep the Spirit at arm's length? Put a checkmark by any of the ones that have ever resonated with you.
>
> ☐ I don't need the Holy Spirit because I have Jesus.
>
> ☐ The Holy Spirit is only for super-spiritual people.
>
> ☐ The Holy Spirit is only for super-strange people.
>
> ☐ The power of the Holy Spirit isn't for us today. It was only for "back then."
>
> ☐ The Holy Spirit doesn't serve a purpose in my life.
>
> ☐ The Holy Spirit is superfluous to my faith.
>
> ☐ The Holy Spirit is only for people who want to exercise spiritual gifts.
>
> ☐ I wouldn't know what to do with the Holy Spirit.
>
> What else would you add?

These are all very common misconceptions about the Holy Spirit that are perpetuated by the enemy. The enemy knows that if we get to know the wonderful friend and companion we have in the Spirit, He will enlarge our hearts for Jesus. He will make Jesus more and more irresistible to us.

He does this by awakening our minds and hearts to what Jesus accomplished for us on the cross. The significance of Christ's sacrifice becomes very real to us when—and only when—the Spirit enlightens the eyes of our hearts to see it. But it goes beyond seeing it. The Spirit makes us bask in the beauty of Christ's love.

THE SPIRIT IS THE DIFFERENCE

Reflect on seasons in your life when your faith has felt dull and dry. Now reflect on times when it has felt alive and flourishing. Can you identify how the Spirit's presence and power made the difference?

Maybe you didn't even realize at the time that the Holy Spirit was the difference maker. That has been one of the sweetest gifts in writing this study—reflecting on and recognizing, oftentimes for the first time, where the Spirit was at work even when I didn't know it.

A life void of the Spirit's active presence and power falls so far short of the dynamic life we were made to experience in Christ. It also doesn't draw others to the gospel because they don't see anything in us that they don't already possess or want.

OPEN YOUR BIBLE and read Ephesians 1:15-23.

In verses 17-19 specifically, Paul prayed that the Father would give us the Spirit, that our hearts might be enlightened, so we will know three things. List them below:

1.

2.

3.

If we neglect the Spirit, who wants to empower us to experience the glory of Jesus, we will settle for:

• A faith frustrated by discontentment;

• Rote religion and stale sentiments; and

• Knowing what we're supposed to believe about Jesus but never experiencing the intimacy of His love.

Do you know the hope to which He has called you? This is the assurance of eternal life guaranteed by your possession of the Holy Spirit.

Do you know the richness of your inheritance? This is the immeasurable riches of His grace in kindness toward us (Eph. 2:6-7)!

Do you know the immeasurable greatness of His power toward you? This is the same extraordinary supernatural power that raised Jesus Christ from the dead!

This is the good stuff the enemy is determined to make us miss out on. The question we have to answer is, *Will I let him win or am I all in?*

WHERE DO WE SHINE THE SPOTLIGHT?

Just as the Holy Spirit's goal is to put the spotlight on Jesus, it's the Holy Spirit in us that makes us want to take the spotlight off ourselves and shine it on Jesus.

The Holy Spirit protects us from wanting glory and honor that belongs to Jesus. A woman who is led by the Spirit is a woman whose life makes much of Jesus. She will not hoard the glory. It will go where it belongs: the name above every other name.

Name a few women or men whose lives glorify Jesus.

What specific things do they do or what traits do they possess that make you more captivated by the greatness of God rather than the greatness of them?

A self-glorifying life is a warning sign that we lack the activity of the Holy Spirit. And a Jesus-glorifying life is a good sign of the Spirit's activity.

But now I want us to think about this as it relates to motherhood.

See, I want my life to be a love song for Jesus. I want my life to testify to the incomparable love of Jesus so that my children will find Him to be irresistible. I bet you do too. But here's the relief. We don't make our lives a love song. The Holy Spirit does. The larger we allow Him to become in our lives, the more beautiful the melody will be.

I think we mamas are good at feeling like we have to be our child's savior and holy spirit. We put so much pressure on ourselves to be who only Jesus can be for our kids and to do what only the Spirit can do in their lives. But the Holy Spirit in us empowers us to turn the spotlight on Jesus, the only One who will never fail them and will always be faithful to uphold His promises to them.

The Holy Spirit's primary purpose is to reveal the glory of Jesus through you, but don't let the devil fool you into thinking this can only happen through your "perfect parenting" or "good days."

We can ask the Holy Spirit to make our lives point to Jesus' perfection when our kids take the brunt of our imperfection, and we can believe He will do it. We can call on the Holy Spirit to make our lives testify to the selfless love of Jesus when our kids encounter our selfishness, and we can believe He will do it. This is what He delights to do.

In what areas do you feel like you fail your children or fall short as a mom?

How can your shortcomings testify to Jesus' perfection?

How can your unrighteousness bring glory to the righteousness of Christ that covers us?

Pause and reflect on where you want to ask the Holy Spirit to shine the spotlight on Jesus through your weaknesses and shortcomings.

Jesus taught His disciples this principle in John 15:26-27. **OPEN YOUR BIBLE** and read those verses now.

What did Jesus say the Holy Spirit will do? And what did Jesus say we must also do?

HOW DOES THIS EMPOWER MY PARENTING?

Jesus affirmed that the ultimate aim of the Holy Spirit is to point people to Him. To testify to who He is and what He accomplished. And then He affirmed how we are to partner with Him in that work: we must testify about Him.

Do you want your life to point your children to His goodness? Good grief, I do! I want it more than anything else, and I bet you do too.

We no longer have to be weighed down by the reality of our weakness or ashamed of the ways in which we fall short at being our child's savior. We were never meant to play that role, and we were never meant to receive that glory. The glory belongs to Him alone.

Let's ask the Holy Spirit together to make His aim our aim. Let's ask Him to lead us into deeper dependency on and intimacy with Jesus. And then let's thank Him again for this glorious reality: The assurance we have in Jesus and the affection we feel for Jesus is produced by the Holy Spirit. Is there any better gift?

#NeverAloneBibleStudy

THE PERSON OF THE HOLY SPIRIT

I'm in a season of parenting that can feel immensely overwhelming. While motherhood is never boring, nor does it ever fail to expose our weaknesses, certain seasons demand more of us than others. Anyone else feel it? I think it's OK to admit when it's a lot.

I also don't think it's a coincidence that I feel this way right now. When I shared how I'm feeling with a wise friend, she suggested the enemy is particularly committed to seeing me feel defeated and unqualified as a mom in hopes that I will shrink back from writing a study about parenting in the power of the Holy Spirit.

Why doesn't the enemy want us doing this study?

Because the enemy doesn't want us encountering God the Holy Spirit in a fresh way! He doesn't want us aware of the authority we have over his head games, and He doesn't want us reminded of the hope we have in Jesus. The enemy's scheme is to keep us parenting alone and in fear. He doesn't want us depending on the supernatural power of God the Holy Spirit in us.

That's why I am so excited about this week, because we are studying how the Holy Spirit is God and why He is so essential in our lives and our parenting.

HE IS GOD

The Holy Spirit is God. Of course, most of us would acknowledge that the Holy Spirit is God without any hesitation. We would agree that God eternally exists as Father, Son, and Holy Spirit. We would happily affirm the doctrine of the Trinity, meaning that Scripture reveals one God who exists in three coeternal divine Persons. And yet, maybe the way some of us live our lives suggests we also believe the Holy Spirit is the optional Person of the Trinity. Or the least accessible. So how has the Holy Spirit become the least acknowledged and most forsaken?

> Why does it matter in your motherhood that you know the
> Holy Spirit is God?

Hold onto that answer and let's open our Bibles to discover just a few of the places where we see the Trinitarian God on display and why it matters for us today. After all, we need to know who He is before we can trust what He does, right?

THE TRINITY IN SCRIPTURE

God eternally exists as three divine Persons: Father, Son, and Holy Spirit. There is one God, and each Person in the Trinity is fully God. The Father, the Son, and the Holy Spirit are inseparable. We can't have faith in God without Christ's sacrifice and then receiving the Spirit. Our faith actually means participating in God's eternal triune life and communion with Him.

I've heard the Trinity called a matter of heavenly mathematics, and for good reason. It supersedes human understanding.

The Trinity is not 1+1+1=3 (one God plus one God plus one God equals three Gods). The Trinity is not 1/3 + 1/3 + 1/3 = 1 (the Father is 1/3; Jesus is 1/3; the Holy Spirit is 1/3). The Trinity is 1 x 1 x 1 = 1 (God the Father, God the Son, and God the Holy Spirit are the One True God).

Let's start at the very beginning of the Bible to explore this.

OPEN YOUR BIBLE and read Genesis 1:1-2.

Who created the heavens and the earth?

Who was hovering over the waters?

Can you picture it? The Spirit was positioned to accomplish what God planned. He was hovering over the water, bringing order and calm to the chaos. (Oh, to think that He hovers over our homes! Desiring to bring calm to the chaos within our walls. Do it, Lord!)

Now let's read John 1:1-3 below.

In the beginning was the Word, and the Word was with God, and the Word was God. He was in the beginning with God. All things were made through him, and without him was not any thing made that was made.

The "Word" was in the beginning, and of course, we know the Word to be Jesus (John 1:14). The descriptions of creation highlight all three Persons—God the Father, God the Son, and God the Holy Spirit—working together in the creation of the world. God is one, and He is three, and it has always been this way.

Millard Erickson is helpful here. He says,

"There have always been three ... and [they] have always been divine. One or more of them did not come into being at some point in time, or at some point become divine. There has never been any alteration in the nature of the Triune God. He is and will be what he has always been."[7]

Let's keep going to highlight just a few of the many more places—in both the Old and New Testaments—where we see the magnificence of a triune God.

"The word for 'spirit' is *ruach* in Hebrew and *pneuma* in Greek. The former is used roughly ninety times for the Holy Spirit in the Old Testament. The latter is employed more than two-hundred-and-fifty times as a reference to the Spirit in the New Testament. Both words can refer to wind or breath. The general idea is the same: *ruach* and *pneuma* express energy, motion, life, activity. The Holy Spirit is God's power and presence among His people."[6]

TRIUNE GOD IN THE OLD TESTAMENT

Circle the word "us" or "our" in each of the verses below.

- In Genesis 1:26, in the creation narrative God said, "Let us make man in our image, after our likeness."

- In Genesis 3:22, during the fall of man the Lord God said, "Behold, the man has become like one of us in knowing good and evil."

- In Genesis 11:7, when the people had become too proud and attempted to build the Tower of Babel to rule over creation, God said, "Come, let us go down and there confuse their language, so that they may not understand one another's speech."

- In Isaiah 6:8, during Isaiah's commission, he heard the voice of the Lord saying, "Whom shall I send, and who will go for us?"

TRIUNE GOD IN THE NEW TESTAMENT

Read Acts 5:3-4 below.

> But Peter said, "Ananias, why has Satan filled your heart to lie to the Holy Spirit and to keep back for yourself part of the proceeds of the land? While it remained unsold, did it not remain your own? And after it was sold, was it not at your disposal? Why is it that you have contrived this deed in your heart? You have not lied to man but to God."

Who did Peter say Ananias lied to in verse 3? In verse 4? What's the significance of this?

Yes, it attests that the Holy Spirit is God. Lying to the Holy Spirit is lying to God. And in John 14:26, we find one of the most profound teachings on the Trinitarian being of God in just one sentence. Jesus said,

> But the Helper, the Holy Spirit, whom the Father
> will send in my name, he will teach you all things and
> bring to your remembrance all that I have said to you.

Jesus said the Father would send the Spirit in the name of the Son.

Because God is so different from us, it can be hard for us to wrap our minds around the way that He works in general, let alone the way that His triune being plays out.

So let's stay with this a little longer to see the triune Godhead revealed throughout the Old and New Testaments. God is always working from the Father, through the Son, in the Spirit, throughout the whole Bible. The Trinity is always working in perfect unity. Here's one example:

Matthew 28:19 says,

> *Go therefore and make disciples of all nations, baptizing them in the name of the Father and of the Son and of the Holy Spirit.*

What is so fascinating is how the Holy Spirit's less emphasized and visible work in the Old Testament and in the Gospels isn't meant to diminish His equality but to create anticipation for Pentecost, when the Spirit would come in fullness and in fulfillment of prophetic promise. Anticipation! I love how our God is a God who creates anticipation. There is always more with Him. We worship a God who says, "Just wait until you see what I will do next!"

Review the following Scriptures to see how God has built anticipation in believers and then fulfills His promises. I've filled in the first one for you.

"The trinitarian structure appears throughout the New Testament to affirm that God Himself is manifested through Jesus Christ by means of the Spirit."[8]

ANTICIPATION	FULFILLMENT
What's the anticipation in Joel 2:28-32? *The Holy Spirit will come upon all of God's people.*	How was this fulfilled in Acts 2? *On the Day of Pentecost, believers were filled with the Spirit and could understand different languages.*
What's the anticipation in Ezekiel 36:22–37:14?	How was this fulfilled in Ephesians 1:13?

What's the anticipation in
Isaiah 11:1-5?

How was this fulfilled in
Matthew 3:13-17?

THE HOLY SPIRIT'S FUNCTION AND PURPOSE

The Holy Spirit carries the same authority and shares the same attributes as God the Father and God the Son, but like all Persons of the Godhead, He is distinct from them, and He performs specific functions.

Fill in the blanks from the paragraph above:

The Spirit carries the same _____ and shares the same _____ but like all of Persons of the Godhead, He is _____ from them and He performs _____ functions.

This is really important and speaks to the tragedy of the Spirit often being neglected and forgotten. God the Holy Spirit does specific work—supernatural work—in exalting God the Son to the glory of God the Father. The Spirit's presence is the manifestation of the Trinity among us today!

Do we believe that? Do we believe that God the Holy Spirit is the One who manifests God the Father's power in our lives? Maybe we need to look in the mirror and remind ourselves at the beginning of each day that the same God who spoke the universe into existence is the One who indwells us by His Spirit.

Now we understand why it matters so much in our motherhood that we know the Holy Spirit is God. We can do hard things as moms—and navigate hard seasons with our children—not because of anything we bring to the table but because God's Spirit in us is more than sufficient for our struggles. The reality of "I can't" brings the relief of "He can!" Nothing is impossible for Him. And everything that is His is ours (1 Cor. 3:21). Not just some things. Not even most things. *Every* thing.

How much pressure do you feel to hold all things together for your children when it feels like it's all falling apart?

How does this pressure impact how you parent?

OPEN YOUR BIBLE and read Colossians 1:15-20.

In whom do all things hold together (v. 17)?

Jesus reconciled us to God, and He reigns supreme over all our earthly struggles. He gives us what we need to face each new day while we rest in the assurance that He has covered what we can't control. But let's be honest. It doesn't always feel that way, right? Sometimes I cry out "Lord, do you really hold all things together? Because right now it feels like you're letting it all fall apart."

How have you witnessed His faithfulness when it feels like things are falling apart?

But there's more. The invisible becoming visible (vv. 15-16) speaks to the gracious nature of God in letting us see the image of God in Jesus' incarnation on earth and in letting us experience the power of God through the testimony of Jesus' life and the Holy Spirit's working in our hearts and minds.

Let's take a moment to think about how this knowledge can impact our kids.

HOW DOES THIS EMPOWER MY PARENTING?

What situations are your children currently facing where they need to know they have the Holy Spirit to help them and empower them?

What we're discovering to be true for us is also true for our kids. The Holy Spirit's power doesn't kick in at a certain age. When our kids believe in Jesus, they have the Holy Spirit.

In the morning, four of my five boys pile into the car for school drop off. First I drop off my two middle schoolers, then my high schooler, and then my preschooler. (Andre is in college and doesn't need a ride!) These days are fleeting, and there isn't anything I would trade for those precious minutes with my kids in the car before school. On the way to school, we open the Bible app and listen to the short story or devotion of the day. It only takes a few minutes, and then I pray for us. But as I have grown in my understanding of and relationship with the Spirit, I have realized how little I've called down the power of God in my morning prayers, and I've become increasingly bolder about asking the Spirit to manifest His presence in them. I want them to know they are never alone, and I want them to experience the empowerment of God as they go about their day. So now I pray boldly for them to know His presence and experience His power. Of course, I can't force any of that in them, but I can surely pray for it. I can plant the seeds of knowledge and expectation.

If your heart is heavy or fearful because your children have not put their trust in Jesus, I want to encourage you to keep praying, believing, and holding onto hope. Also, invitational language with our unsaved children can be helpful. "This is why I pray for you to believe in Jesus. So you will be saved from the penalty of sin, freely given eternal life, and experience God's great love and power in your life today!"

We can encourage our children in every trial or fear they face: "You have the Holy Spirit! You are never alone in anything you go through. When you feel afraid, when you face temptation, when you feel left out, when your heart feels sad, when anxious thoughts fill your mind, God's power is inside you through His Spirit. Nothing is impossible for Him, and everything He has is yours!"

Where do you see windows of opportunity to weave this good news into conversations or situations with your children?

Fellow mom, God the Holy Spirit is alive and accessible to you today. Live like that's true, tell it to your children, and live in anticipation of what He will do.

DAY 2
HE IS EQUAL

Think with me about how parents typically introduce their children. For instance, when introducing her children, does a mom say, "Hi, this is Tommy. He is our middle child, but he is the most important child in our family. This little guy is little Teddy. He is next in significance to me, but he was born last. And this is our firstborn, Minnie, but I introduce her last because, well, she is the least special in our family."

Could you even imagine?

The order in which parents name their children doesn't represent their significance in the family. It represents the revelation of the children into the parent's lives.

Where am I going with this? It's been suggested, and many assume, that because the Holy Spirit is the last to be named in the Trinity, and because His work is last to be emphasized in Scripture, He is least in significance in the Godhead. But that couldn't be further from biblical truth.

I confess that my analogy falls a bit short because the Father, Son, and Holy Spirit are eternal, so they didn't come into being like our children. But I hope it helps you think about the Holy Spirit's equality in a fresh way.

Today we will discover how the order in which we say God the Father, God the Son, and God the Holy Spirit when speaking align with the way they exist. The Father begets the Son. The Son is begotten of the Father, and the Spirit proceeds from the Father and the Son. We may see the Bible order the Father, Son, and Spirit differently from passage to passage for different purposes, but it's important for us to know that God's being is eternal from the Father, to the Son, and Holy Spirit.

EQUALITY OF THE TRIUNE
Let's take a look at both the Old Testament and New Testament for more context on their equality.

Look up Deuteronomy 6:4 and write it below.

This central verse of Israel's faith teaches us that there is only one God.

Now turn to the New Testament and read The Great Commission in Matthew 28:18-20. Jesus said the disciples should baptize people in the name of whom?

Now read the three verses below, and as you do, pay attention to the commonalities in what Jesus said each time.

And I will ask the Father, and he will give you another Helper, to be with you forever.
JOHN 14:16

But the Helper, the Holy Spirit, whom the Father will send in my name, he will teach you all things and bring to your remembrance all that I have said to you.
JOHN 14:26

But when the Helper comes, whom I will send to you from the Father, the Spirit of truth, who proceeds from the Father, he will bear witness about me.
JOHN 15:26

Based on these three verses, answer the following questions:

Who will the Father send?

At whose request will the Helper be sent?

What are some of the things the Helper will do?

There is one God with one being who is distinct in Persons and performs distinct functions. The Holy Spirit is one of the three Persons, equal with the Father and the Son, and yet, so often as Christians, we neglect the Spirit's significance and forfeit benefiting from His distinct function in our lives and our parenting.

> Is this similar to or different from how you've thought about the Holy Spirit's equality in the Trinity? Explain.

HE IS INDISPENSABLE

If we lack attention to and affection for the Spirit's distinct function in our lives, we will be left powerless to live life to the fullest, which Jesus came to give us. Our faith will flourish to the extent that we are fueled by the Spirit. Our lives will produce the fruit of the Spirit to the extent that we are filled with the Spirit.

Why does this matter for us as moms today? Because if we treat Him as the least significant, we forgo the supernatural work He wants to do in our lives. He is indispensable in us becoming more of the moms we long to be!

- If we want to be more patient with our children when we are tested beyond our limits, we need the Holy Spirit to manifest His patience in us. **Read Galatians 5:22-23**, and record how these verses speak to our need for the Spirit in this situation.

- If we want to have more hope about our children's futures when we see them making foolish choices, we need the Holy Spirit to make hope abound in us. **Read Romans 15:13**, and record how this verse speaks to our need for the Spirit in this scenario.

- If we want to show more joy in our homes when people are unpleasant or days are just downright hard or circumstances are exhausting, we need the supernatural joy that comes from being filled with the Holy Spirit. **Read Acts 13:52**, and record how this verse speaks to our need for the Spirit in our homes.

> Have you longed to be more patient? More hopeful? More joyful? What else do you need more of? Be specific.

Based on what we've learned today, how significant is the Spirit to you experiencing "the more"? Explain.

BUT I ALREADY HAVE JESUS!

One of the questions Francis Chan poses in *Forgotten God* is, "I've got Jesus. Why do I need the Spirit?"[9]

Pause here and answer that question based on what you've learned so far.

Yes, we have all we need in Jesus in the sense that there is nothing that can supplement His perfect work on the cross to rescue us and secure our eternal salvation. *He is life!* I can wholeheartedly say there is absolutely nothing better than the love of Jesus. He is the sole remedy for our sin-sick hearts and the fulfillment of everything we long for.

But, remember, Jesus Himself said it was better that we have the Holy Spirit because He would be God's power and presence among us and in us after Jesus ascended to heaven (John 16:7-11). Before receiving the Spirit, the cross and resurrection are just things that happened in the past. If the Spirit doesn't indwell us, then we don't have Jesus. But once we receive the Spirit, Jesus' work is made real for us in the indwelling of the Spirit. The Holy Spirit is the One who helps us work out the salvation and the full life that Jesus secured for us. He is not "instead of;" He is "because of."

In your own words, describe the difference in the Holy Spirit being "because of" rather than "instead of."

He continues the work that Jesus started!

This is the undeniable truth witnessed on the Day of Pentecost and throughout the Book of Acts: We need the power of the Spirit to unite us to Christ and then propel the gospel of Christ. And while we are called to do this in our world, the holy work begins in our homes.

> Do you ever feel frustrated or discouraged by the holy work you seek to do under your own roof? Meaning, do you wonder if any of it is making a difference or will really reap a harvest? Why or why not?

Of course, as Christians, we may say "knowing I'm saved is enough for me," but goodness do we settle for less than everything God has planned for us when we miss out on having earthly impact for the kingdom and leading our children to do the same.

Gosh, I do. Often! I can get easily discouraged by the lack of interest any one of my kids might show in spending time with God or by the lack of fruit I see manifesting in their lives. But I find renewed enthusiasm in remembering that the power of the Spirit is at work in the seeds I plant in ways I can't even fathom. This is the truth I have to go back to over and over again.

HE IS EQUALLY AVAILABLE

The Holy Spirit is not only eternal like the Father and Son, but He is also equal with the Father and Son. And not only is the Spirit equal to the Father and the Son, the Spirit is as equally available as the Father and Son.

OPEN YOUR BIBLE and read Romans 8:9-11,14.

Jesus' death and resurrection reconciled us to God, giving us full access to the throne of grace through the Spirit. Then Jesus' ascension ushered in the Holy Spirit's coming and granted us full access to the Spirit.

When you put your trust in Jesus, you get to be led by the Spirit. He is fully available to you today!

But how does all that Christ accomplished become ours? The Holy Spirit is our unbreakable bond to Christ. And this is just as true for the mom who was raised in a Christian home and has been reading her Bible her whole life as it is for the mom who just began following Jesus.

This is what we need to know: He is equally available to every Christian. He doesn't avail Himself to us once we reach a certain point in our Christian walk. He doesn't activate His life-changing power based on how long we've been following Christ. In fact, we're only Christians because the Spirit is available to us.

But this we also need to know: equally available doesn't mean equally active. Uh-oh, that wasn't fun to read.

> Describe in your own words the difference in the Holy Spirit being available to you and being active in your life.

HOW DOES THIS EMPOWER MY PARENTING?

We have to yield to the Spirit's leading to walk in obedience to Christ if we want to experience the full measure of the Spirit's power. Isn't it interesting how the world feeds us the lie that God gives us instructions (or commands) on how to live because He wants to steal all the fun and freedom from our days? But nothing could be further from the truth, and this is such an important message for our kids.

> Children often correlate obedience to our rules as something that prohibits a free life. As an adult, how do you reconcile your freedom with being obedient to God's instruction?

Living in accordance with the Word of God is what activates the power of God. And what is more exciting than experiencing the power and presence of God? We are too easily pleased by the lesser things. Meanwhile, God wants to free us from slavery to the sins that the enemy uses to destroy us. Once we recognize this, obedience doesn't feel like an obligation. In fact, we quickly discover that the sacrifice of obedience produces a spiritually plentiful life.

DAY 3
HE IS PRESENT WITH US

We don't hear much about the Personhood of the Holy Spirit, which is why I am so excited about what we'll unpack today, because knowing the Holy Spirit is a Person is foundational to our faith. His divine Personhood is what invites us to enjoy a deeply personal friendship with Him.

When Jesus promised the disciples He would send the Holy Spirit to them after He left them, Jesus said, "And I will ask the Father, and he will give you another Helper, *to be with you forever*, even the Spirit of truth. ... [H]e dwells with you and will be in you" (John 14:16-17, emphasis mine). The Holy Spirit has an ongoing, active presence in the life of every believer. What great news for us! We are never alone, because we have the constant companionship of the Holy Spirit!

THE SPIRIT'S PERSONALITY

The Christian life is dependent on the presence and work of the Holy Spirit in our lives; it's only through the Spirit that we become Christians in the first place and that we continue to grow in Christlikeness (our sanctification). This is why Jesus assured: "It is to your advantage that I go away, for if I do not go away, the Helper [the Holy Spirit] will not come to you" (John 16:7). Because the Spirit plays such a critical role in our lives and spiritual growth, shouldn't we desire to grow in our knowledge of Him? Thankfully, the Bible paints a clear picture of the Spirit's personality to help us better understand Him.[9]

One primary barrier to enjoying the Holy Spirit's friendship is the misconception that He is a mere symbol rather than a divine person. He is often mistaken for the things by which He is symbolized in Scripture, such as a dove (Mark 1:10), fire (Acts 2:2-3), or a flowing river (John 7:37-39). Each of these symbols carry beautiful significance and are visual images that help us understand how the Spirit works in our world and our lives, but He isn't confined to any of the symbols.

Look up the following verses and fill in the blanks as you read.

Romans 8:27 (CSB): "And he who searches our hearts knows the _____ of the Spirit, because he intercedes for the saints according to the will of God."

1 Corinthians 12:11 (CSB): "One and the same Spirit is active in all these, distributing to each person as he _____."

Ephesians 4:30 (CSB): "And don't _____ God's Holy Spirit.
You were sealed by him for the day of redemption."

The Spirit can be grieved, which demonstrates He has emotions. Just think about the emotions of Jesus on display throughout the Gospels. These emotions are experienced by the Father and the Spirit. In summary, the Holy Spirit is a divine Person who demonstrates for us the mind, will, and emotions of our one true God.

> Did you know how relational He is? How does this change
> or influence the way you think about Him or relate to Him?

Recognizing that He has a dynamic personality changes how we relate to Him, right? He isn't an "it" or a symbol. He is a divine Person with whom we can have a relationship. But let's not miss this: being in relationship with Him is not the same thing as being yielded to Him. Just like you can hurt a friend or a child or a spouse, you can hurt the Holy Spirit. It remains true that you can never lose Him or be abandoned by Him, but you can grieve Him and diminish the sense of His presence in your life.

Today I want us to hone in on the Spirit's emotions and how we can grieve Him. Knowing I can hurt Him in how I parent my children has only increased my desire to deal gently with my children.

GRIEVING THE HOLY SPIRIT

When someone is grieving, it means he or she is experiencing deep sorrow resulting from loss, but loss doesn't have to mean death. It can be the loss of a bond where deep affection and connection once existed.

This is what Paul addressed when he wrote in Ephesians 4:30,

> *And do not grieve the Holy Spirit of God, by whom*
> *you were sealed for the day of redemption.*

The Greek word for "grieve" in Ephesians 4:30 is *lupeō* and it can mean "to make sorrowful; to affect with sadness, cause grief; to throw into sorrow."[10] How do we hurt the Holy Spirit? Paul answered that question in verse 31:

> *Let all bitterness and wrath and anger and clamor and*
> *slander be put away from you, along with all malice.*

> Circle the words above that teach us what makes the Spirit sorrowful.

Let's use this time to get really honest with the Friend who will never forsake us. This exercise isn't about informing the Spirit where we struggle. He already knows! It's about coming clean with ourselves, which is the beginning of change.

Which of the behaviors in verse 31 hit home for you today? Explain why.

BITTERNESS AND ANGER IN MOTHERHOOD

One thing you can count on with me is honesty about my need for help. The grace of God frees me to tell you where I struggle because I know His grace not only covers my sin, it changes my heart—however slow that work might sometimes seem. Bitterness and anger are two areas where I struggle. I didn't know how angry I could get until I became a mom. I didn't know how hard it would be to respond gently when my children chose blatant disobedience.

Is this resonating with you? I'm not who I was, but to say I never let my anger win or hold onto hard feelings for too long would be a lie.

Oh, Jesus, thank You that You never give up on us or stop shaping us into Your image. We have such hope in Your faithfulness.

The Holy Spirit sorrows over our sin, and in this case, we are talking about the ones we commit against each other, including our kids. There is an undeniable relational theme in the list Paul laid out in Ephesians 4:31.

Acting out in anger or holding onto bitterness are the things we do because we feel like we have a "right to" or because we just "want to." When our kids are disobedient and disrespectful and drive us straight to the edge of crazy, we are inclined to react in ways that don't reflect the character of Christ. We are rebellious sinners parenting rebellious sinners, so of course it's going to be messy. (Rebellious sinner isn't our identity of course, but it's the reality of our fallen nature.) And yet, somehow, if you're anything like me, you can get good and angry when parenting isn't going the way you want it to, which is tidy and pretty.

But this is the truth that is changing me and making a difference in my parenting: When we grieve the Holy Spirit, our bond of unity and connection with Him is interrupted. He is *that* sensitive to our willful sin because He knows how our sins impact our relationship with God, bring sadness to our own souls, hurt our human relationships, and specifically in this context, damage the bond of affection we have with our children.

The consequences of our sin run both vertical and horizontal.

We know the guilt and shame that come soon after we lose it with our kids. Ugh. We know how painful the clean-up of our harsh words and condescending tone can be. We know how awful it feels to sit in the aftermath of our anger and wish we could take back every unloving word spoken because of how deeply and completely we love our kids.

> What behaviors in your children or circumstances in your home most tempt you to respond in a way that grieves the Spirit? Spend time with this, because identifying triggers is instrumental to the change the Spirit wants to bring.

If this is stirring anything up in your spirit, I'd encourage you to confess it, repent of it, and just quietly sit in the Lord's presence, because He wants you to sense His love and forgiveness washing over you and cleansing you. There is so much forgiveness here.

FORGIVE ONE ANOTHER

The Message paraphrase of Ephesians 4:30 is so poignant:

> *Don't grieve God. Don't break his heart. His Holy Spirit, moving and breathing in you, is the most intimate part of your life, making you fit for himself. Don't take such a gift for granted.*

So we know what not to do, but as the gospel always does, it never leaves us in the don't column. So then, what are we to do if we don't want to grieve the Spirit and hinder His work? Paul goes on to give us the answer.

> Read Ephesians 4:32 and record what brings delight to the heart of God and restores intimacy with His Spirit.

Think about this: kindness and gentleness are fruit of the Spirit. This means the Spirit manifests His character in us and through us. The opposite of what grieves Him is what He grows in our lives. We don't do this alone. We have the supernatural power within us to respond to our children in a way that pleases God.

The Message paraphrase of verse 32 says it this way:

> *Forgive one another as quickly and thoroughly as God in Christ forgave you.*

What is most difficult for you about this instruction?

HOW DOES THIS EMPOWER MY PARENTING?

One thing that helps me choose gentleness and tenderness when my flesh flares up is praying that the Holy Spirit would bring the gospel to remembrance. We will soon study this essential function of the Holy Spirit, but for now may I offer just a few of my prayers in case they might be helpful to you today?

Holy Spirit, when I want to get angry over my child's sin, help me remember how patient and slow to anger God is with me when I am disobedient.

Holy Spirit, when I want to hold onto bitterness over my child's behavior, help me remember how much Jesus has forgiven and rescued me.

Holy Spirit, when I want to respond to my child's rebellion with a harsh tone, help me remember how tenderhearted and kind God is with me, even on my worst day.

What specific prayers would you like to include here?

The good news is that everything we need to respond in kindness to our children and to keep intimacy with the Holy Spirit is possible through His supernatural empowerment. We will see, in the days ahead, even more of how He gives us the grace—the power—to choose grace-filled responses with our kids.

DAY 4
HE IS OUR GUARANTEE

We recently put our house on the market, and our real estate agent staged our bathrooms with beautifully folded washcloths, fancy soaps, and brand new electric toothbrushes. Well, the night after our first set of showings, I walked into the boys bathroom after they'd gone to bed to discover they'd washed their hands with the fancy bar of soap, dried their hands with the washcloths, and made the "display" toothbrushes their own. Can you relate?

If you've ever been through the home selling process, you know how valuable the buyer's down payment is. If you go through the trouble of hiding many of your belongings in the closest so your home is staged for potential buyers to imagine themselves in it, getting all of your people out of the house at the drop of a hat to show it, and then weighing the pros and cons of offers from potential buyers, you know that without the down payment, their offer brings no relief. But with the down payment comes the assurance that they will fulfill their promise to purchase your home.

What does this have to do with the Holy Spirit's power in our parenting? God didn't purchase a home with cash. He purchased a people (you and me) with the life of His Son. And to a much greater degree, the Holy Spirit is the down payment, the guarantee of what's still to come.

The Holy Spirit is our ...

- proof of our present condition of salvation;

- promise that the fullness (or wholeness) of our inheritance in Jesus will be received; and

- pledge that our salvation will be completed through glorification.

WE ARE HIS CHILDREN

OPEN YOUR BIBLE and read Ephesians 1:1-14, but before you do, I'd like to encourage you to read it aloud and insert the word "me" whenever you come to the word "us," and "I" whenever you come to "we." Paul has written a beautiful summary of our spiritual blessings in Christ, and I think it behooves us to personalize it today and ask the Holy Spirit to awaken us to the magnificence of it.

> When you finish reading, record what bubbled up inside you, or what the Holy Spirit awakened in you.

I want to share with you what the Holy Spirit highlighted for me when I read this passage in the New Living Translation. It was three words: "as his own." I was working on this chapter while sitting in a small, bleak waiting room while my son took a three-hour test, and even there, the Holy Spirit arrested my heart with those three words, and tears of gratitude filled my eyes.

Let's read verses 13-14 (NLT) together:

> *And now you Gentiles have also heard the truth, the Good News that God saves you. And when you believed in Christ, he identified you as his own by giving you the Holy Spirit, whom he promised long ago. The Spirit is God's guarantee that he will give us the inheritance he promised and that he has purchased us to be his own people. He did this so we would praise and glorify him.*

> Fill in the blanks below:
>
> *How did God identify you as His own? By giving you the _____ _____, just as He promised.*
>
> *The Holy Spirit is God's _____ that He will give us the inheritance promised us.*
>
> *He did this so that _____.*

When we believe in Jesus, God calls us His own. "Mine." We are marked in Christ with a seal—the promised Holy Spirit. We are God's cherished and chosen possession. I still get undone by this truth. I am God's daughter, a daughter of the King, covered in the righteousness and perfection of Jesus Christ, sealed by the Holy Spirit as a sign that He will finish what He started in me. He will finish what He started in you. And He will finish what He started in our children.

When I lay my head on my pillow, rehearsing all the ways I'm afraid I let my God down again in my parenting (I raised my voice too much, I skipped morning devotions with them, I wasn't present enough, I lacked joy, and the list goes on), I am assured that the Holy Spirit is the guarantee that God won't give up on me, as rebellious as I can be. The Holy Spirit is God's guarantee that we will inherit all of the spiritual blessings in Christ—and His purpose is the praise of His name. Like we discovered earlier in our study, this affirms that the Holy Spirit's aim is to bring praise to the Father and the Son.

Paul wrote something similar about the Holy Spirit in 2 Corinthians 1:20-22:

> *For all the promises of God find their Yes in Him [Jesus].*
> *That is why it is through him that we utter our Amen to God*
> *for his glory. And it is God who establishes us with you in*
> *Christ, and has anointed us, and who has also put his seal*
> *on us and given us his Spirit in our hearts as a guarantee.*

Circle where you see the assurance of your anointing in 2 Corinthians 1:20-22 above.

Every promise of God is fulfilled in Jesus. Every prophecy in the Old Testament is fulfilled in Jesus. And today, every longing of the human heart is fulfilled in Jesus.

Then God places His Spirit in us and puts the seal of His Spirit on us to help us live in confidence of everything that is ours in Jesus.

Have you feared that your past mistakes or the sins you commit on a daily basis will keep you from eternal life? Or maybe you're more worried about being excluded from God's goodness in the here and now. Explain.

In what areas of parenting do you fear you're disappointing God or failing as a parent?

What confidence do you gain from knowing that nothing you've noted above keeps God from welcoming you?

When we become Christians, our very being is united to Christ. His life is our life. His death is our death to sin. His resurrection is our resurrection. We can't be separated from Jesus because we are "in Him."

> *Who shall separate us from the love of Christ?*
> *Shall tribulation, or distress, or persecution, or famine,*
> *or nakedness, or danger, or sword? ... For I am sure that neither*
> *death nor life, nor angels nor rulers, nor things present*
> *nor things to come, nor powers, nor height nor depth,*
> *nor anything else in all creation, will be able to separate*
> *us from the love of God in Christ Jesus our Lord.*
>
> **ROMANS 8:35,38-39**

I have spoken with many mamas who have watched their kids launch into the world with Jesus, but they don't keep walking with Jesus on their journey. Though most of our prodigal sons and daughters come home, the waiting can be excruciating. Watching our kids walk outside the will of God is so painful because we know what they're forfeiting—the peace, the love, the purpose, the joy. The truth we can have confidence in as we wait is that the Holy Spirit remains in our kids and His seal remains on our kids, even when they wander.

If you have a child who has wandered, take time now to ask the Holy Spirit to make Jesus irresistible to your child again. Call down the loving conviction and invitation of the Spirit in his or her heart.

Now is probably a good time for us to talk about a passage that has been known to breed much fear and confusion among Christians.

BLASPHEMY AGAINST THE SPIRIT
OPEN YOUR BIBLE and read Matthew 12:22-32.

Now let's read verses 31-32 together. Jesus said in no uncertain terms,

> *Therefore I tell you, every sin and blasphemy will be forgiven people, but the blasphemy against the Spirit will not be forgiven. And whoever speaks a word against the Son of Man will be forgiven, but whoever speaks against the Holy Spirit will not be forgiven, either in this age or in the age to come.*

We might read that and ask, *How can Scripture teach that the Holy Spirit is my seal of security of salvation but also teach that blaspheming the Spirit will never be forgiven me?* I am hopeful we are about to have clarity about what Jesus was teaching and gain greater confidence in the seal of the promised Holy Spirit.

So what does it mean to blaspheme the Holy Spirit?

The ESV Gospel Transformation Bible says,

> *"Blasphemy against the Holy Spirit is the unchanging conviction that Jesus is evil. In essence, the only unforgivable sin is a conclusive rejection of Christ rather than a contrite reception of Him."*[11]

The seal of the Holy Spirit identifies us as God's possession and guarantees our eternal security in Christ. If we bear this seal, we never—ever—have to fear committing the unforgivable sin of blasphemy.

> *"In light of the gracious heart of God as revealed throughout Scripture, and in light of the doctrine of eternal security (e.g., John 10:28-30), we can say that if a person is concerned that he may have committed the 'unforgivable sin,' this concern is proof that he has not committed it. There would be no concern if the Holy Spirit had ceased conviction. Anyone who desires God's forgiveness for anything will receive it. Therefore, the only truly unforgivable sin is one for which the sinner refuses to seek forgiveness."*[12]

Any fear that God will stop calling us His possession if we don't have perfect performance is put to rest in the Holy Spirit's presence.

HOW DOES THIS EMPOWER MY PARENTING?

Fear that God will stop calling our child His own when doubt creeps into their hearts or when they wrestle with uncertainty that leaves them questioning is put to rest in the Holy Spirit's assurance. We are one in Him now, and He cannot disown Himself:

> *If we are faithless, he remains faithful—for he cannot deny himself.*
> **2 TIMOTHY 2:13**

What fears is God inviting you to lay before Him, trusting that the Spirit is working in your life and in your children's lives?

We can be absolutely confident that on the days when we seek Him with all our heart, as well as on the days when we wander off like lost sheep, the Spirit promises we will receive everything He has for us because of what Jesus did for us.

This is a powerful message we can pass down to our kids, especially the ones who are good at being hard on themselves. The seal of the Holy Spirit is the security of their salvation.

#NeverAloneBibleStudy

THE POWER OF THE HOLY SPIRIT

One of the things that settled on me in a fresh way as I began to study the Holy Spirit is what we will unpack this week—and that is how the Spirit of Christ is the same Holy Spirit who lives within believers today. As we learn about the power of Jesus on display during His earthly ministry, it's incredible to think how, through our relationship with Jesus, we now live in the power of the Spirit of Christ!

That realization led me to this question: *Why do I try to accomplish anything apart from His power?*

I find it so fascinating how even when we know that our best effort falls so short of what the Spirit can do, we're still prone to go it alone.

This reminds me of a hilarious story I recently heard about a friend of mine.

Her mom recounted how, when she was a little girl, she was playing in a sand box and lost a jack she was playing with. The longer she searched, the more upset she got, as she began to lose hope that she'd recover her toy. It was then that her mom said, "Honey, why don't you pray and ask God to help you!" So that is what her daughter did. She prayed out loud, "God, please help me!" It wasn't much later that she recovered her jack. As soon as she recovered her toy, she prayed aloud again. But this time she said, "Never mind, God, I found it!"

Goodness, I find myself in her story. We try to go about it in our own wisdom and strength, but then we remember how much we need God's help, and even then, we struggle to recognize His work in our lives or praise Him for it. We go right back to "I've got this!"

Tracing the evidence of the Spirit's power that we see so clearly through Jesus' work during His time on earth has profound implications for us as moms, as we will see this week. So today we will take a high-level look at the Gospels to see what we can learn about how the power of the Spirit is at work in and through us.

DAY 1
HE EMPOWERED JESUS

OPEN YOUR BIBLE and read Luke 1:35.

What is the work of the Holy Spirit in this passage?

OPEN YOUR BIBLE and read Matthew 3:13-17.

What happened when Jesus came up from the water?

This passage of Scripture gives us one of the clearest glimpses of our triune God. The dove as the symbol of the Holy Spirit shows us that the Spirit is the bond of love between the Father and the Son. Even when Jesus became human, He did not surrender His divinity, His communion with the Father and the Spirit.

But there is something else wonderful happening here. Record below what the voice from heaven said.

Are you someone who has lived under the pressure to perform for God's pleasure? Oh Mama, lean in.

I'm going to speculate that God was being very intentional in His timing of declaring His love and pleasure in this moment in time. He didn't wait to announce His love and pleasure over Jesus after He overcame every temptation and performed miracles and defeated the grave. Jesus' eternal Sonship alone made Him pleasing to God, not to mention the fact that as a human being he was sinless. And this is how the Father now loves us when we are covered in Jesus' righteousness. God's pleasure in us isn't performance-based. It's Jesus-based.

We not only have the same power in us that raised Jesus Christ from the dead; we also have the same pleasure of the Father because of our relationship with Jesus. Good parenting doesn't make us more pleasing to God, and poor parenting doesn't make us less pleasing. We please the Father because the perfection of His Son covers us.

Before we move on to how Jesus ministered in the Spirit, I also want us to note how the Gospel of John attests to the work of the Spirit in the baptism of Jesus:

> *Then John gave this testimony: "I saw the Spirit come*
> *down from heaven as a dove and remain on him."*
> JOHN 1:32, NIV

What does John say the Spirit did when He came upon Jesus in the form of a dove?

By using the word "remain," John revealed another important piece of the story, which is the permanence of the Spirit's anointing presence in Jesus' life and service as Messiah. Why does the word "remain" matter? I'm no bird expert, but one thing I've learned about doves is that they are particularly skittish birds, and they are quick to flee at any interruption to peace. Yet the dove that descended upon Jesus felt right at home in His holiness and perfection.

Unlike our lives that can grieve the Holy Spirit, causing the dove's activity to diminish, the Holy Spirit's activity in Jesus' life would never be interrupted, because Jesus and the Spirit are one. This means Jesus' ministry was continually accomplished through the power of the Spirit.

I love how Peter spoke to this truth in Acts 10:37-38 (NIV):

> *You know what has happened throughout the province*
> *of Judea, beginning in Galilee after the baptism that John preached—*
> *how God anointed Jesus of Nazareth with the Holy Spirit and*
> *power, and how he went around doing good and healing all who*
> *were under the power of the devil, because God was with him.*

What did God do? What did Jesus do?

What about this surprises you or encourages you?

POWER TO FACE TEMPTATION
OPEN YOUR BIBLE and read Luke 4:1-2.

Who was Jesus full of?

Who was Jesus led by?

Jesus ate nothing for forty days while being tempted by Satan to sin. Can you even imagine? I have trouble defeating Satan's temptation to sin before my kids even make it out the door for school in the mornings—with a full stomach and a full cup of caffeine in my hands. What might be on display is my impatience with their inefficiency getting ready or maybe a complaining tongue about the housework that always needs to be done.

But Jesus, faced with Satan determined to see Him fall to sin, defeated him. Yes, Jesus knows what it feels like to be faced with relentless temptation, but He never succumbed.

Keep reading through verse 13.

In each of the three temptations you just read, how did Jesus defeat Satan?

Jesus countered each temptation from Satan with the Word of God, which Paul referred to as "the sword of the Spirit" in Ephesians 6:17. The Holy Spirit inspired men to write down the words of Scripture (2 Pet. 1:20-21), and this same powerful piece of armor is ours to take up in the battle against Satan that we continue to fight today. Jesus acts in the power of His own Spirit, the Holy Spirit. Through our union with Him, we can now live in the power of the Spirit of Christ. Mama, you are equipped to defeat Satan!

Let's not miss how John concluded in verse 13.

> What did Satan do after he was done tempting Jesus in the wilderness?

He didn't depart for good. He departed only until he saw another opportunity to tempt Jesus.

When Peter warned, "Your adversary the devil prowls around like a roaring lion, seeking someone to devour" (1 Pet. 5:8b), he wasn't exaggerating Satan's commitment to destroy us. The devil is persistent in his pursuit to see us succumb to sin or live under a shameful narrative of lies. But I don't say this to scare us; I say this to encourage us to do what Jesus did.

We have the power of God's Spirit inside us and the power of God's Word to guide us! Through every temptation we face and every boldface lie Satan wants to plant in our minds, we already have the victory. That should motivate us to engage in the fight. It should also make us wonder why we would ever pass up such power by neglecting the Holy Spirit's presence in our lives.

> Where do you feel under attack? What false beliefs about your identity are bombarding you? What temptation is Satan using to try and take you down?

> How have you been fighting back? What changes do you need to make to fight as Jesus did?

POWER FOR MINISTRY
OPEN YOUR BIBLE and read Luke 4:14-21.

Look again at verse 14 and record below the words that reveal how Jesus returned to Galilee.

Jesus, in the power of the Spirit, had the courage to stand before the violent opposition and proclaim Himself as the Son of God who would bring salvation.

From this moment on we see Jesus preaching and performing miracles to the full extent of His power.

Read the verses below and list the miracles Jesus performed in each text.

- Matthew 12:28

- Luke 8:22-56

- John 2:1-11

- John 5:1-18

- John 6:5-14

- John 6:16-21

- John 9

- John 11:1-45

- Acts 10:37-38

Jesus is God, and even during His time on earth He had the full power of His Spirit in Him. When He left, He sent that same Spirit to live in and operate through us. We aren't casting out demons under our roofs, but Jesus is still in the business of performing miracles—and that includes miracles in our kids' lives. Goodness, did I need to be reminded of that today, because we could use some wonder-working power under our roof right now! Jesus is still in the business of doing good and healing the oppressed and sick.

Where do you need a miracle right now under your roof?

Sometimes we can be afraid to ask for a miracle because we don't want to be left disappointed, but I believe God's invitation to us today is to know His wonder-working power in a fresh way. Let's go boldly before the throne of God, Mama! We can adopt the same posture Jesus did in the garden of Gethsemane: *I know you can! I pray you would. Your will be done!*

POWER OVER DEATH

Not only do we see the power of Jesus' Spirit during His earthly life but also in His death.

> Underline in each of the passages below where you see mention of the Spirit.

How much more will the blood of Christ, who through the eternal Spirit offered himself without blemish to God, purify our conscience from dead works to serve the living God.

HEBREWS 9:14

For Christ also suffered for sins once for all, the righteous for the unrighteous, that he might bring you to God. He was put to death in the flesh but made alive by the Spirit.

1 PETER 3:18, CSB

... And was declared to be the Son of God in power according to the Spirit of holiness by his resurrection from the dead, Jesus Christ our Lord.

ROMANS 1:4

HOW DOES THIS EMPOWER MY PARENTING?

If the Spirit of him who raised Jesus from the dead dwells in you, he who raised Christ Jesus from the dead will also give life to your mortal bodies through his Spirit who dwells in you.

ROMANS 8:11

Write in your own words what Romans 8:11 means for you as a mom.

We've said it already but it's worth saying again: The same Spirit of Jesus dwells in you! Right here. Right now. He lives in *you.* He will give life to your mortal body, but He will also breathe life into the weary and tired places on the daily. Let Him do it!

HE GAVE POWER TO JESUS' DISCIPLES

I'm still working on becoming friends with the word *wait*. I'm guessing you might relate. When we have good work we want to do, or ideas we believe will benefit the kingdom, or dreams we want to see come to fruition, waiting can feel like a waste of time. I've gotten myself into all manner of trouble and missed out on God's best for my life when I've moved forward with my plans even though my spirit knew God was saying, "Child, wait." It really comes down to trust, doesn't it? Do I trust that He is good and is good to me?

What is perhaps even harder than waiting for God to show His power in our own lives is waiting for God to show His power in the lives of our children. Right? I've lost count of the number of times I've advised the Lord on how He needs to intervene sooner and work faster in the hearts of my boys. "Show your power, Lord!" is my prayer on repeat. And I'm still learning to lean into waiting when I want to take things into my own hands.

> Can you identify a time when it seemed like the Lord was slow in keeping His promises to you or your children? In looking back, what evidence do you see that the Lord was present and working while you were waiting?

HE'S ALIVE!
Jesus' disciples were no strangers to waiting on God to fulfill His promise.

OPEN YOUR BIBLE and read John 14:16-31.

This is probably Jesus' most significant teaching on the Trinity, and we've looked at some portions of it already in our study. In this passage Jesus promised the power of the Holy Spirit to His disciples—power that would literally change everything for them. See, Jesus knew His death was imminent, so He began preparing His disciples for the work of the Holy Spirit in their lives. He assured them that the same presence and power that was with Him would soon be given to them.

We will be spending several more days studying John 14 and its teachings about the work of the Holy Spirit, but for now, let's fast-forward to when the resurrected Jesus (who had just endured the cross, defeated death, and rose from the grave) briefly appeared to His disciples.

OPEN YOUR BIBLE and read Luke 24:36-49.

Post-resurrection Jesus appeared to the disciples, enjoyed a meal with them, reminded them they were witnesses to Him fulfilling everything that was written about Him, and then He concluded with a very important instruction.

What did Jesus tell His disciples to do in verse 49?

The last recorded instruction of Christ in the Gospel of Luke—before He was taken to heaven—was Jesus telling His disciples, "Wait! Don't even think about trying to do the work of the Father without the power of the Spirit" (my paraphrase).

Just after Jesus instructed His disciples to wait to witness until they'd received God's power,

> [He] ... led them out to the vicinity of Bethany, [and] he lifted
> up his hands and blessed them. While he was blessing them,
> he left them and was taken up into heaven. Then they
> worshiped him and returned to Jerusalem with great joy.
> And they stayed continually at the temple praising God.
> **LUKE 24:50-53, NIV**

Based on the verse above, what did they continually do at the temple?

They praised while they waited. They were expectant about being filled with the same Holy Spirit that they saw at work in Jesus. Their posture was praise, and their prize was power.

This passage concludes the Gospel of Luke, and then Luke opens the Book of Acts with a refresher on how Jesus promised the coming of the Holy Spirit.

OPEN YOUR BIBLE and read Acts 1:1-8.

Jesus specifically said two things would happen:

Record below what Jesus said in verse 5.

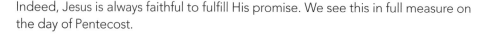

In verse 8, what did Jesus say would be the result of being baptized?

Indeed, Jesus is always faithful to fulfill His promise. We see this in full measure on the day of Pentecost.

THE DAY OF PENTECOST

Pentecost is one of three major Jewish festivals that occurs fifty days after Passover and celebrates the end of the grain harvest. Believers had gathered to celebrate the Pentecost that followed Jesus' death and resurrection, which occurred ten days after Jesus' ascension into heaven and fifty days after His resurrection. At 9 a.m., the Holy Spirit was unleashed, filling 120 people, including the disciples, and each one received the supernatural power of God that forever changed how we experience God's power. It's a power that continues to defy human understanding and supersede human strength.

Pentecost was the day God poured out the Holy Spirit not just *onto* but *into* His people, ushering in a new experience of unforeseen power that continues today. Jesus' followers in the upper room were given the permanent presence and power of the Holy Spirit through their faith in Jesus. The story unfolded in the most dramatic way:

*When the day of Pentecost arrived, they were all together in one place.
And suddenly there came from heaven a sound like a mighty rushing
wind, and it filled the entire house where they were sitting.
And divided tongues as of fire appeared to them and rested on each
one of them. And they were all filled with the Holy Spirit and began
to speak in other tongues as the Spirit gave them utterance.*

ACTS 2:1-4

What happened once the disciples were filled with the Spirit?

There was nothing subtle about Jesus' sending the Holy Spirit. A mighty wind rushed through the room. Tongues of fire flickered over their heads. Then the 120 men and women began speaking in a number of different languages. "Other tongues" means they were all empowered to speak other known and recognizable languages they had not previously known how to speak.

The gospel was no longer bound by language or ethnic barriers.

God was so intentional in His timing! Check this out: The Holy Spirit descended on a day when devout Jews from every nation annually gathered in Jerusalem. And when the God-fearing Jews heard the commotion in the upper room they came running to see what was happening. In doing so, they were all able to hear the gospel being preached in their own language and bore witness to the mighty work of the Holy Spirit (Acts 2:5-11).

The good news of salvation in Jesus was now accessible to every nation and language. The triune God ordained it and enabled it! But not everyone who bore witness to it believed it or liked it. (Sounds a lot like our world today.)

Pentecost was such a joyous and profound moment that those who bore witness to it couldn't help but have a strong reaction to it. Many were amazed and curious:

*"They are speaking of the powerful works of God to all of us
in our own language! … What can this mean?" But others
laughed and made fun, saying, "These men are full of new wine."*

ACTS 2:11-13, NLV

But Scripture tells us these people weren't overcome by wine; they were overcome with the Spirit of God. And they were about to light the world ablaze with the good news.

> Why would some of the onlookers be displeased with the joy they witnessed?

The power the disciples needed back then is the same power we need now. We need the Holy Spirit to do the holy work of God in our homes. We need the power of the Spirit to impart the wisdom of the Spirit. We need the power of the Spirit to have the joy of the Spirit.

HOW DOES THIS EMPOWER MY PARENTING?

We best bear witness to Jesus in the power of His Spirit. And here's the great news: because of Pentecost, we get to! Jesus did not tell us to wait for the Holy Spirit to fill our homes like the disciples had to wait for the Holy Spirit to fill the upper room. We have His indwelling right now.

Whatever the work of your hands may be today—whether it's playing an imaginary game with your toddler, calming the fears of an anxious teenager, tidying the house after the kids go to bed, or sneaking back into their rooms after they've fallen asleep to whisper a prayer and kiss their foreheads—remember that the Holy Spirit now dwells in you and empowers you. He wants to fill your home with His presence and fill your spirit with His contagious joy. Amen!

> In closing, write a prayer of thanksgiving for how the Spirit is available to you now.

DAY 3

HE WORKED MIGHTILY THROUGH THE DISCIPLES

I think it's fair to wonder if we can really enjoy and experience the Holy Spirit like the early church did. Maybe we wonder if there was something special about the disciples that we don't possess, like a strength of faith or a track record of obedience, and therefore the power they experienced isn't one that will ever be activated in our lives. Or maybe we assume that the Holy Spirit only moved with that kind of power "back then."

It's OK to have these questions, but I'm hopeful we'll see today how much we have in common with the 120 who received the Holy Spirit. They were men and women, fathers and mothers. They were disciples who had doubts, and they were followers with faults and plenty of failures. But what they all had in common was they made themselves available! They wanted God's power activated in their lives.

Let's pick up where we left off yesterday.

PETER'S CHANGE OF HEART

In response to the accusation of day drinking, Peter stood up with a new boldness and began to preach salvation to the skeptical crowd.

This is no small thing if we remember who pre-Pentecost Peter was. From the moment Jesus called this fisherman to follow Him, Peter struggled to faithfully trust and testify to Jesus. Peter cared deeply about the opinions of others and was labeled a coward for denying Jesus three times before Jesus was crucified.

But now we see a forgiven Peter. A reinstated Peter. A grateful-for-grace Peter. A fearless Peter. An empowered Peter.

> Take a moment to read all of Acts 2. Then we'll hone in on some key verses.

Full of the Holy Spirit, Peter was the first to stand and preach a legendary sermon about salvation being available to all men and women, both Jew and Gentile, young and old: "Why do you seem so surprised about what you see? This is precisely what the prophet Joel said would take place, people!" (my paraphrase).

After Peter recited the Old Testament prophecy about God pouring out His Spirit on all people (Acts 2:16-21), he concluded,

> "Exalted to the right hand of God, [Jesus] has received from the Father the promised Holy Spirit and has poured out what you now see and hear. ... Therefore let all Israel be assured of this: God has made this Jesus, whom you crucified, both Lord and Messiah."
>
> ACTS 2:33,36, NIV

I can only imagine the passion with which Peter preached the bold words, "Be assured of this!"

Post-Pentecost Peter was utterly fearless in proclaiming the name of Christ in the face of adversity. His life is the prime example of the radical change that occurs in a person who has been baptized with the Spirit of God.

Read Acts 2:37-41 below to see how the crowd responded.

> ³⁷Now when they heard this they were cut to the heart, and said to Peter and the rest of the apostles, "Brothers, what shall we do?" ³⁸And Peter said to them, "Repent and be baptized every one of you in the name of Jesus Christ for the forgiveness of your sins, and you will receive the gift of the Holy Spirit. ³⁹For the promise is for you and for your children and for all who are far off, everyone whom the Lord our God calls to himself." ⁴⁰And with many other words he bore witness and continued to exhort them, saying, "Save yourselves from this crooked generation." ⁴¹So those who received his word were baptized, and there were added that day about three thousand souls.

Fill in the blank from verse 37 above:

Now when they heard this they were _____ ____ _____ _____,
and said to Peter and the rest of the apostles, "Brothers, _____
_____ ____ ___ ?"

It wasn't Peter's persuasive speech that caused them to be convicted; it was hearing the gospel preached in the power of the Holy Spirit.

What was Peter's response to their question in verse 38?

Look again at verse 38. Did Peter say "you *will* receive" or "you *might* receive"?

This answer is the same for us today. Repent and receive!

For whom did Peter say was the promise in verse 39?

Maybe you have children who feel "far off." Maybe you're afraid you are too far off. This promise is for you. It's for your children. There are no exceptions. There is no place we can run that His promise can't reach. The baptism of the Holy Spirit is a gift to all who repent!

How many more repented and were baptized that day?

OPEN YOUR BIBLE and read Acts 3:1-16.

As people gathered in amazement over the healing, notice how Peter responded:

> *"People of Israel," he said, "what is so surprising about this?*
> *And why stare at us as though we had made this man*
> *walk by our own power or godliness?"*
> ACTS 3:12, NLT

> *"Through faith in the name of Jesus, this man was*
> *healed—and you know how crippled he was before.*
> *Faith in Jesus' name has healed him before your very eyes."*
> ACTS 3:16, NLT

Peter used this display of power to point to Jesus and assure the crowd that none of his miraculous works were because of his own power or godliness. Peter's aim was to point people to Jesus alone. It wasn't for his own personal gain and glory.

How does Acts 3:1-16 speak to your role as a mom?

What is your aim as a mom?

What is your motive for wanting to parent in the power of the Holy Spirit?

The power of the Holy Spirit is meant to help us live like Jesus and point people to Jesus, giving all to the glory of God.

If our motive to seek the Spirit's power is to be above others rather than to better love others, we've gotten it all wrong. If our motive in wanting the Spirit's power is for anything less than our witness, we've missed the purpose of the power. God gives us His power as we live out our purpose for the praise of His name!

Not having the same experience as the 120 doesn't mean God hasn't started something that can be fanned into flame as our faith increases and our faithfulness to His Word grows. Even if we don't observe the power of the Holy Spirit at salvation as tangibly as the early church did on Pentecost, that doesn't mean it's off limits to us. It means there's always more of God for us to experience.

Let's pause here to dig into the power that fell on Pentecost. See, you may not have begun speaking in other languages when you repented and received Jesus. You probably didn't run into the street and preach a powerful sermon to your neighborhood when the Holy Spirit took up residence in you. I certainly didn't do either of those things when the Holy Spirit opened my heart to Jesus at eight years old. In fact, I didn't even realize I was given the incredible gift of the Holy Spirit in that moment. I prayed. I cried. I snuggled into my mom's arms and felt the enormous weight of my sin lifted. But I did not consciously welcome the Spirit's work in my life until much later in my walk with Jesus.

Parenting in the power of the Holy Spirit is about being empowered by the Spirit to parent in the likeness of Jesus so that God may be glorified in our homes. We need the power of the Holy Spirit to parent with the fruit of the Spirit.

We may not be healing beggars by the temple gate but our daily doings are no less of an opportunity for our children to see the Holy Spirit powerfully working through us.

I want my whole life to make much of Jesus. I bet you do too. The way I make a PB&J, the way I toss laundry into the washing machine, the way I respond to people who cut me off in traffic (still very much working on this one!), and the way I respond when I'm inconvenienced by my children—I want all of it to be done in the power of the Holy Spirit.

> What situations in your daily parenting can be opportunities for the Holy Spirit's presence to be made known in your home?

Here's the thing. Parenting in the power of the Holy Spirit isn't something we do. It's something that's done in us and through us.

Consider again at what Peter said: "We didn't do this in our own power or godliness. Only faith in Jesus can do this" (my paraphrase). With faith in Jesus comes the indwelling power of the Holy Spirit who works in us and through us to the glory of the Father.

FULL OF THE SPIRIT
Soon after Peter's legendary sermon, Peter and John were seized and thrown in jail for the night. Meanwhile the number of believers grew to about 5,000 (Acts 4:4).

Did this make Peter cower? We might expect it would but it did not. It only fueled him. The following day Peter and John were questioned by the angry opposition.

OPEN YOUR BIBLE and read Acts 4:7-8,11-12.

As you read through the Book of Acts, you'll notice how often Luke wrote the phrase "filled with the Holy Spirit" or "full of the Holy Spirit" when writing about the acts of the disciples. This reminds us that the acts being accomplished weren't the acts of people. These were acts of the Holy Spirit through very ordinary people. And the crowd was captivated by them because of who dwelt in them.

The Message paraphrase puts Acts 4:13-14 this way:

[The crowd] couldn't take their eyes off them—Peter and John standing there so confident, so sure of themselves! Their fascination deepened when they realized these two were laymen with no training in Scripture or formal education. They recognized them as companions of Jesus.

"Companions of Jesus." Doesn't that have the sweetest sound. Oh, how I want my life to testify to my being in Jesus' company. *Lord, let it be so.*

How can we be "companions of Jesus" today?

A lot of us feel inadequate to teach our kids the gospel. Maybe you didn't grow up in a Christian home where it was modeled for you so you don't have an example to emulate. Maybe you don't feel like you know the Bible well enough to teach it to your kids.

What else, if anything, feels like a stumbling block to discipling your kids?

Peter's testimony is exhibit A of the Holy Spirit's power to transform weakness into strength, fearfulness into courage, timidity into boldness, impulsiveness into self-control, foolishness into wisdom, and a pattern of failure into resounding eternal success.[14]

When we read that Peter and John were two "laymen with no training in Scripture or formal education," what confidence can we gain from knowing the Holy Spirit who empowered them is the same Spirit who lives in us to help us disciple our kids, both in word and deed?

Peter and John were ordinary men, but they had the extraordinary power of the Holy Spirit. How they lived their lives made the power of the Spirit irresistible to those who witnessed it.

STEPHEN'S INDICTMENT

As the disciples continued to preach the gospel with boldness throughout Jerusalem, the charges against them continued to mount. They were accused of seeking to abolish the Mosaic law and destroy the temple. As a result, Stephen, one of the seven men added to the disciples to preach the good news, was seized. But rather than recoil, Stephen, full of the Spirit, delivered an epic retelling of how Jesus was the fulfillment of the law. Then he concluded with the following:

> *You stiff-necked people! Your hearts and*
> *ears are still uncircumcised. You are just like*
> *your ancestors: You always resist the Holy Spirit!*

ACTS 7:51, NIV

What do you think Stephen meant when he said they "always resist the Holy Spirit"?

How might you be resisting the Spirit?

The language of "stiff necked" traces back to what God said of the Israelites throughout the Old Testament. God constantly likened them as "stiff necked," an expression used of stubborn cattle. "Stiff-necked"—or "stubborn" (AMP) or "bullheaded" (The Message)—is an ancient problem, not something new, creative, and unique to them then, or to us now! It's an ancient problem presented in new ways.

We might not reject Jesus as the righteous One or persecute prophets, but we're good at hushing the Holy Spirit and resurrecting idols of the heart that compete with our affection for and delight in God. Maybe it's Netflix®, booze, food, approval, or shopping.

Let's take a moment to ask God to reveal any idols that didn't come to mind when we assessed whether we resist the Spirit. Now let's receive His forgiveness and ask Jesus—the resurrected One—to take His rightful place in our hearts.

This is why we need the Holy Spirit to keep wooing our hearts back to Jesus by continually revealing the beauty of Jesus and reminding us He is better than all our false loves. And only by the power of the Spirit are we enabled to fight the substitutes we put in God's rightful place.

Stephen's indictment infuriated the religious leaders, but Stephen didn't stop there. He continued to proclaim the gospel of Jesus Christ with boldness.

> But Stephen, full of the Holy Spirit, looked up to heaven
> and saw the glory of God, and Jesus standing at the right hand
> of God. "Look," he said, "I see heaven open and the
> Son of Man standing at the right hand of God."
> ACTS 7:55-56, NIV

> They covered their ears and, yelling at the top of their voices, they all rushed
> at him, dragged him out of the city and began to stone him. Meanwhile,
> the witnesses laid their coats at the feet of a young man named Saul.
> ACTS 7:57-58, NIV

> While they were stoning him, Stephen prayed, "Lord Jesus,
> receive my spirit." Then he fell on his knees and cried out, "Lord,
> do not hold this sin against them." When he had said this, he fell asleep.
> ACTS 7:59-60, NIV

As Stephen, full of the Spirit of glory, breathed his last breath, he prayed that the Father would forgive his persecutors like Jesus prayed the Father would forgive His persecutors on the cross.

Did you notice in verse 58 who witnessed Stephen's confidence as he was stoned to death? Write his name here:

In a dramatic moment the camera pans over to Saul, who is watching this unfold, doing what he thinks is right in God's eyes, but it's not long until the Holy Spirit gets ahold of Him too. Yes, this is the same notorious Saul, who was the relentless and barbaric persecutor of Christians. This is the same Saul who, just two chapters later, would have his own transformative experience with Jesus and "be filled with the Holy Spirit" (9:17) and immediately proclaim "Jesus in the synagogues" (9:20). This is the same Saul, whom we now call Paul, who penned most of what we'll read in the New Testament about the Holy Spirit. God is so creative and redemptive.

HOW DOES THIS EMPOWER MY PARENTING?

Do you know what that means for us today? Our past is no match for God's grace. If Saul, a self-proclaimed "foremost" of sinners (1 Tim. 1:15), can be reconciled to God through Jesus, be filled with the power of the Holy Spirit, and become one of the most influential instruments in spreading the gospel, then we never have to doubt if we can experience this same grace and power today in our homes!

DAY 4

HE GIVES POWER TO US

Knowing we have the power of the Holy Spirit is radically different than knowing how to live by the power of the Holy Spirit, and I think this is where a lot of us struggle. We know we are supposed to rely on the Holy Spirit, but we don't know how to avail ourselves of His power.

I don't think most of us avoid living by the power of the Holy Spirit intentionally. I just think He seems inaccessible to a lot of us, and the actual ability to draw on His power feels unattainable. But whatever the reason, we too often neglect to take hold of the benefits of the divine Person who resides inside us.

HOW DO I RELY ON THE SPIRIT'S POWER?
Corrie ten Boom said,

> *"Trying to do the Lord's work in your own strength is the most confusing, exhausting, and tedious of all work. But when you are filled with the Holy Spirit, then the ministry of Jesus just flows out of you."*[13]

Those are some good words to describe how it feels to parent in our own power, aren't they? Confusing—check. Exhausting—check. Tedious—check.

But when we yield to the person of the Holy Spirit, the power of the Holy Spirit within us will flow from us.

We will kick off next week with how our spirit is filled with the Holy Spirit, and specifically, what it means to enjoy His presence. But today, let's camp out in the important truth that we indeed have the ability to live in the power of the same Holy Spirit who fell upon the 120 at Pentecost and what that means for us as moms.

OPEN YOUR BIBLE and read Galatians 3:1-15.

How did Paul say we *receive* the Spirit? (See vv. 2-3.)

Then, in verse 14 (NIV), Paul wrote,

> *He redeemed us in order that the blessing given to*
> *Abraham might come to the Gentiles through Christ Jesus,*
> *so that by faith we might receive the promise of the Spirit.*

Underline where Paul reiterated how we *receive* the Holy Spirit.

Now let's look at verse 5 (NLT), where Paul addressed how we *live* by the Spirit:

> *He redeemed us in order that the blessing given to*
> *Abraham might come to the Gentiles through Christ Jesus,*
> *so that by faith we might receive the promise of the Spirit.*

Underline how Paul said we *live* by the Spirit.

Read Galatians 3:6 again. What did Abraham's belief produce?

What Paul revealed is that we live by the power of the Holy Spirit (and become vehicles for Him to work) in the same way we first received the power of the Holy Spirit: by believing the message of Jesus Christ—the gospel!

And in case we aren't clear, Paul emphasized this teaching in Galatians 3:3 (NLT) when he asked the Galatians,

> *How foolish can you be? After starting your new lives in the Spirit,*
> *why are you now trying to become perfect by your own human effort?*

How were they trying to become perfect?

Feel familiar? Trying to become perfect in my own strength sure sounds familiar to me! Maybe we should pause and ask ourselves the same question as it relates to how we parent.

Why do we strive to become perfect Christian parents by our own human effort when we have the power of the Holy Spirit to make us more like our perfect Savior?

The Holy Spirit is our only hope for becoming who God has created us to be and parenting the way He has called us to parent. He gives us power to do what we can't do on our own.

Of course, this doesn't mean we do nothing. It doesn't mean we don't have to obey God's commands to grow in God's character. The Spirit doesn't excuse our effort. He empowers our effort.

Now consider how Galatians 3:5-6 is written in The Message:

> Answer this question: Does the God who lavishly provides you with his own presence, his Holy Spirit, working things in your lives you could never do for yourselves, does he do these things because of your strenuous moral striving or because you trust him to do them in you? Don't these things happen among you just as they happened with Abraham? He believed God, and that act of belief was turned into a life that was right with God.

Read that passage again and answer the following questions. (This is so vital to the rest of our study because every part of the Christian life is powered by the Spirit.)

Does God lavishly provide His Spirit or does He give us bits and pieces of His Spirit?

What does God do for us that we could never do on our own?

Does God work out His character in our lives based on how hard He sees us trying to modify our behavior or because we yield to Him and trust Him to do so within us? Said another way, is God's work in our lives based on our trying or our trusting?

Based on what we just read in Galatians, answer this question in your own words: *How do you parent in the power of Holy Spirit?*

Mama, you have the ability to live in the power of the Holy Spirit. Yield to Him and trust that He will guide you in all your ways.

LIVING FULL OF THE SPIRIT

Now that we've seen how often Scripture specifically says "full of the Holy Spirit," I want us to reflect on how we are "full of the Holy Spirit."

Write your name first on the line below, and then write some of the things you do throughout your day. Be specific. Don't hold back. (The point of this exercise is to comprehend being indwelt by the Holy Spirit and that you can be filled by Him, just like Jesus' early disciples. And just like the disciples did everything through His power, so can you.)

_____, full of the Holy Spirit, _____
_____
_____
_____
_____.

These are the things we do. Now let's ask ourselves if we do them with the same characteristics as the disciples.

Think back to some of the common characteristics that were on display for others to see when the disciples were full of the Holy Spirit. Two that very clearly jump out to me are boldness (Acts 4:31; 14:3; Eph. 6:19) and joy (Acts 13:52; John 16:13-24). They were bold in sharing the gospel, and they were full of joy as they did it.

BOLDNESS

Mamas, our families need us to be bold with the gospel in our homes. Bold doesn't mean aggressive or argumentative. Bold means confident in our hope and courageous in our speech.

> When you think about being bold with the gospel in your home, what comes to mind?

I've heard mamas say things like they are afraid to pound their kids with religion because that will make their kids more resistant. But this isn't about forcing them to believe something. On the contrary, we have good news to give! We know what will quench their thirsty souls. We have life-giving truth to share. Jesus wants to have a loving relationship with us. He wants to give us dynamic and flourishing lives. The enemy will tell us to keep these truths to ourselves because sharing them runs the risk of our kids rejecting it because of us, but those are lies meant to keep the good news of salvation in Jesus from being passed down from generation to generation. Our kids need to hear the gospel and see it lived out by us daily.

It's true that we don't hold the power to produce faith or fruit in our kids' lives; the Spirit does. But we get to partner in that work by being bold with our witness. And He produces that in us.

> In what areas of your parenting do you need the Holy Spirit to embolden you? Take time to ask Him to do that now.

JOYFULNESS

Meanwhile, the disciples were joyful despite the fact that they knew persecution and humiliation and incarceration and even death were awaiting them. They were on mission. The Holy Spirit filled them with boldness and joy to spread the gospel.

> What's your joyfulness meter like these days?

I recognize there might be temptation to feel guilty if your joy meter isn't spiking. So before we move on I want us to acknowledge that life can be hard. Parenting can be hard. And it's natural not to feel joy when our hearts are heavy. But the joy we're talking about isn't natural. It's supernatural. It's joy the Holy Spirit manifests in us. I also want to encourage us to fight for joy, even when circumstances don't feel joyful. (I am writing this while walking through things that do not feel joyful at all. So I am writing this for myself as much as I am writing this for anyone else.) But I am worshiping my way through it. I am tracing my finger over God's faithfulness in the past. And I am begging the Holy Spirit to give me His joy for my children to witness.

> How do you find joy and gratitude in the midst of your endless tasks as a mom or in circumstances that feel heavy and hard in your home? Why does this matter?

HOW DOES THIS EMPOWER MY PARENTING?

I regularly ask myself, *Do my kids know I delight in them like the Father delights in me, or do my kids feel like an inconvenience to me?* This is the supernatural work the Holy Spirit wants to do in us: empower us to meet the needs of our families with glad and grateful spirits.

Today, you and I are on mission in our motherhood. We are on mission in our homes, neighborhoods, workplaces, and PTAs to spread the good news of Jesus Christ. And so I'll say it again: the Holy Spirit who fell on Pentecost is the same Holy Spirit who wants to fill you now with power to use you as a vehicle through which other people—starting with your children—will have their hearts wooed to Jesus and the gospel over and over again.

To be honest, I wish there was a checklist for parenting in the power of the Holy Spirit, because then it would feel like I had more control over how He works in my life. Ah, there it is—it's about control. I want to know that if I check certain boxes, I'm guaranteed His manifested power. But that's not how our relational God works. He says, *Spend time with Me, store My living Word in your mind, and make your heart a welcoming home for My Spirit.* It's about marinating in His presence, not checking the boxes.

That's the good stuff we'll kick off with next week!

#NeverAloneBibleStudy

THE LEADERSHIP OF THE HOLY SPIRIT

The Holy Spirit stirred my heart to repentance the night my mom took me to see the Billy Graham movie *The Prodigal* at a theater in Deerfield Beach, Florida. My motivation for going to the movie with my mom wasn't receiving salvation. It was getting a bag of Twizzlers® and a soda. But my heart was so convicted by the Spirit in that theater that when we got home, I crawled into bed, overwhelmed with certainty of my need for Jesus. I remember the moment my mom walked into the bedroom to find me under the covers. When she leaned down to kiss me goodnight, I asked her to pray with me. I told her I wanted to put my trust in Jesus and accept Him as my Savior.

Since that moment, I have lived in the confidence that I am saved from condemnation for my sins, and that I am freely given abundant and eternal life in Christ.

Everyone who trusts in Jesus as their Lord and Savior receives the gift of eternal life that can't be earned by anything we do or don't do. We all "fall short of the glory of God" (Rom. 3:23). There is absolutely nothing we can do to add to or subtract from the work of Christ on our behalf. It's all grace. This is the salvation narrative—the good news that changes lives. But what I didn't fully understand on that life-changing night of my childhood was the gift I was given in the indwelling Holy Spirit.

Salvation happens in our lives when we repent of sin, believe in Jesus Christ as the only Son of God sent to die on the cross for our sins, and commit to follow Him as the risen Lord from that day forward. At that moment the Holy Spirit comes to live in our hearts, joins us to Christ, and bestows us with all the benefits of our eternal inheritance. It's this filling of the Spirit that equips us to live as faithful believers. It's how God has chosen to help us walk out our faith and share His love with others.

From the moment of salvation on, our ability to grow in our relationship with Jesus and impact the world in His name is dependent on the Spirit.

DAY 1
HE FILLS US

I enjoy making my home a loving place for my family and a welcoming space for friends. I'll get inspiration from home decorators on Instagram® or watch my favorite show, *Fixer Upper*, and then spend more than I intended at Target® to refresh the feel of my home. (Still waiting for the Holy Spirit to manifest the fruit of self-control in the Magnolia section.) A new pillow here, a new plant there, and several new candles of course.

Perhaps you also enjoy making your home a lovely place to dwell. This hobby, if you will, can lead us to a helpful question about our lives in Christ: Are we committed to making our hearts a lovely and welcoming place for the Spirit to dwell like we're committed to making our homes a lovely place for friends and family to dwell?

Making our hearts a lovely dwelling place can be likened to welcoming His leadership in our lives. He longs to flood every room in our heart and lead us in the way of Christ. The Bible describes this leadership as being "filled with the Spirit" (Eph. 5:18). Today we'll consider what that means and how we are to live in response.

WHAT IT MEANS
In the Bible we read about two ways the Spirit fills believers—initially at conversion and ongoing throughout a Christian's life. First, let's consider that initial filling.

> **OPEN YOUR BIBLE** and read John 3:1-15.

> Note each mention of the Spirit in John 3:1-15. Now write your understanding of what it means to be "born of the Spirit."

When Jesus explained salvation to Nicodemus, He emphasized the Spirit's work in a person's conversion using the language of spiritual rebirth. Essential to that rebirth is being "born of the Spirit" (vv. 6,8). The Holy Spirit initiates our relationship with Jesus, then comes to dwell permanently in us.

However, being given the Holy Spirit at salvation is not the same as being continually filled with the Spirit after conversion. Yes, we miraculously become home to the Holy Spirit at salvation and receive the benefits of His presence, but it doesn't always follow that we welcome the outworking of those benefits in our daily lives or in our parenting. That brings us to the second type of filling, and the one we will focus most of our attention on today.

OPEN YOUR BIBLE and read Ephesians 5:15-18.

To "be filled with the Spirit"—as Paul instructed in verse 18—is to be under the influence of the Spirit.

Unlike alcohol, which deadens part of the brain and makes us less aware of reality, the Spirit enlightens our minds to the benefits of belonging to Jesus and empowers us to live the full and fruitful life promised to us in Christ. Sadly, many Christians forgo the supernatural power God provides, the limitless benefits He bestows, and the fruit He manifests because we don't heed Paul's command to be filled and live under the influence of the Spirit.

> On a scale of 1-5 (with 1 being not at all and 5 being all in), where would you say you land in living under the influence of the Spirit? Explain why you chose the number you did.

The original Greek word used for "be filled" in this verse is *pleroō*, which Paul gave as an imperative, or a command.[14] This means that to "be filled with the Holy Spirit" wasn't suggested as an optional part of our Christian walk; it was commanded. Paul wasn't being bossy here; rather, he was reminding us that being filled and empowered by the Spirit is how God designed us to live. In fact, it's the only way to live a faithful and fruitful Christian life.

> How does your feeling about being filled with the Spirit change when you think about this as a command and not a friendly suggestion?

In addition to being a command, this type of Holy Spirit filling is something we are to seek continually. A repeated experience. On the daily. We can go to the Lord with nothing but an empty cup and ask Him to fill us with His Spirit, and He will do it over and over again. Isn't that great news?

HOW TO LIVE FILLED

When it comes to living out Paul's command to "be filled with the Spirit," unfortunately there is no set formula for us to follow. But there are biblical principles for welcoming and activating the Spirit's power in our lives. Let's look at five of those together.

1. **Confess.**

   OPEN YOUR BIBLE and read 1 John 1:9.

   What two things did John say will happen if we confess?

When we live filled with the Spirit, we quickly learn that the Holy Spirit and our sin are not friends. Confess any sin the moment He brings it to mind. Don't hold onto it. He is convicting you of it so you can be cleansed of it. We don't have to worry that our confession of sin will lead to rejection. God is faithful to forgive!

Make it a daily practice to ask the Spirit to reveal the following types of sin, and then confess them when He does:

- *Known sin*: the things you know you did but shouldn't have done and the things you should have done but didn't do.

- *Unknown sin*: the areas in our lives where we don't even realize we are rebelling.

- *Sins of self-righteousness*: areas where you've convinced yourself you're "good enough" and don't need God's grace, or where you have been smug about your sin, or where you attempted to satisfy God's holy demand with good works.

Read Romans 10:3 and 2 Corinthians 5:21 for clarity on why we need to confess self-righteousness.

Because "the human heart is the most deceitful of all things" (Jer. 17:9, NLT), we need the Holy Spirit to help us get honest about our sinfulness.

God may even use trusted friends to bring to light aspects of our lives that need to be reoriented. In a sense, the Spirit uses other believers to convict us of sin and lead us to confession. This shows both the individual and corporate aspect of the Spirit's involvement in our lives.

This is something we can—and need—to do for our children. We can't play the Spirit's role in inclining their hearts toward godliness, but we can help them understand what's going on in their hearts when they choose rebellion.

> Think for a moment about your parenting. How do you respond when your child confesses a mistake to you? Do you view your child's confession as something done for your sake, his or her sake, or something else?

Our children often run and hide instead of willingly confessing when they mess up. They fear consequences, scolding, or even disappointing us. Yet more often than not, we want to turn their mistakes into teachable moments by giving forgiveness, correction, and a change of course. We know we can't transform our children's hearts and make them desire honesty (that's the Holy Spirit's job), but there is something powerful we can do. Like I just mentioned, we can help our children understand what's going on inside their hearts when they sin. We can teach them that their sin never changes God's love, or ours, for them! They can choose to hide their sin and let shame fester in their hearts (a terrible consequence indeed), or they can confess their sin, receive forgiveness, learn from the consequences, and walk in freedom.

David wrote in Psalm 24:4-6: "The one who has clean hands and a pure heart, who does not trust in an idol or swear by a false god. They will receive blessing from the LORD and vindication from God their Savior. Such is the generation of those who seek him, who seek your face, God of Jacob."

Similarly, our exercise of confession leads to forgiveness. We want to be purified. We want to be free from shame. We want restoration with our Father. We want to make our hearts a welcoming home for the Holy Spirit.

OPEN YOUR BIBLE and read Psalm 139:23-24.

Write this prayer in your own words.

Without fear of rejection, ask the Spirit to search and expose the sin that stands in the way of you being filled with the fullness of God.

2. **Repent.**

   OPEN YOUR BIBLE and read Acts 3:19-21.

The word "repent" comes from the Greek word *metanoia*, which means "to have a change of heart."[15] Repentance is about more than feeling sorry for our sin or regretting the consequences of our actions. It's a deep sorrow for wrongdoing that leads to an internal change of heart and mind. A turning back.

When I don't feel genuine sorrow for my sin, I ask the Spirit to break my heart over my sin. I ask Him to tenderize my heart to the price Jesus paid on the cross. This isn't about wanting to feel ashamed of myself over my sin. It's about not wanting to be prideful about the seriousness of it. But there's something else significant about repentance that we often overlook.

> Read Acts 3:19-21 again but pay specific attention to verse 20.
> What does repentance bring about? Times of what?

> What area in your life needs refreshment right now? What aspect of your parenting needs refreshing through repentance?

> Can you see the parallel here with what Jesus said in John 7:37-39? The One who leads us to repentance is also the One who refreshes us! Our days are spent in countless tasks taking care of others. Mama, lean into Him for renewal and refreshing.

3. **Yield.**

    OPEN YOUR BIBLE and read Galatians 5:16-17.

    What jumps out at you in this passage?

We have to yield our self-centered wills to God's authority if we want to be filled. As humans we have a conflict within ourselves to yield to the flesh (sin) or yield to Christ. We live in the tension between freedom to choose how we live our lives and accountability to God for responsible living (Rom. 14). Living through the Spirit, yielding to His work in our hearts, requires us to lean into the empowerment of the Spirit. We have to submit our lives to the way of Jesus and say, "All I am and all I have is Yours to use." And this has to be more than lip service. When we "walk by the Spirit," it allows God to activate His power in our lives. He enables us to obey despite the struggling and suffering this world can bring. For God's power to be active in our lives, we must yield to the Spirit, who guides us in doing God's will.

    How can you model yielding to the Spirit for your children?

4. **Abide.**

When Jesus says, "Abide in me" (John 15:4), He is calling us to stay attached to the vine (Him!) through His life-giving Word, prayer, and a heart of worship. Abiding in Christ means setting aside time to strengthen our relationship with Him. It means reading and applying Scripture to our lives. It means keeping the lines of communication open through prayer and listening for His still, small voice in the midst of a world filled with noise. Mama, we need to know this: If we think we can live fueled by the Spirit without being filled with the Word of God, we are fooling ourselves.

Consider the similarities in the following passages:

> Be filled with the Spirit, addressing one another in psalms and hymns and spiritual songs, singing and making melody to the Lord with your heart.
>
> EPHESIANS 5:18-19

> Let the word of Christ dwell in you richly, teaching and admonishing one another in all wisdom, singing psalms and hymns and spiritual songs, with thankfulness in your hearts to God.
>
> COLOSSIANS 3:16

We know that God's Word is "living and active" (Heb. 4:12), so putting the Word of God inside our minds and hearts is a very practical and powerful practice. (Tomorrow we will look closer at the Spirit's vital role in this.)

In what ways are you cultivating your relationship with God?

What's one new way you can make Bible study, prayer, and worship a normal and daily occurrence with your children to help them practice a life of abiding?

5. Ask.

If you've received Christ, then you've been saved and filled with the Spirit of God. You have the power within you to live a fruit-filled life and lead your children to do the same. But are you asking Him to help you meet the needs you have? If your house is anything like mine, then you've got plenty of requests for God.

OPEN YOUR BIBLE and read Luke 11:11-13.

We are a sinful, self-centered people, but even so, we have a deep desire to give good gifts to our kids.

Fill in the blanks with what Jesus said in verse 13:

*"How much more will the heavenly Father give the _____
_____ to those who _____ him."*

Jesus said to ask! Ask to be filled, again and again, with the Holy Spirit. Fresh filling. So what are we waiting for? Let's ask Him to continue filling us with His Spirit. And then let's walk according to it.

HOW DOES THIS EMPOWER MY PARENTING?

No matter where you are spiritually at this moment, the filling of God's Spirit is for you! Do you feel like you're failing miserably at the Christian life? The Holy Spirit wants to fill you. Do you have doubts or fear about who the Holy Spirit is? He wants to fill you. Are you struggling with sin and carrying shame? The Holy Spirit wants to fill you. Are you overwhelmed with the stress of parenting or stuck knowing how to help shape the children God's given to you? The Holy Spirit wants to fill you. And get this: The more we are filled with the Spirit, the more we will see the character of Jesus manifested in our lives and through us in our homes.

In closing today let's spend time taking inventory of where we might be impeding the filling of the Holy Spirit. Reflect on the following questions and record your thoughts below: *Am I seeking forgiveness for my rebellion, or am I asking the Holy Spirit to coexist with unrepentance? Am I yielded to God's authority, or is my submission more lip service? Am I filling up on His living Word, or am I trying to fuel my life with the things of this world?*

As a believer, you have been filled with the resurrection power of God (Rom. 8:11). There is no limit to what God can do in and through a mama yielded to and continually filled with His Spirit!

DAY 2

HE AUTHORED THE BIBLE

A common way to describe the words of Scripture is "God-breathed," but I wonder if we've ever paused to consider the magnitude of this.

> What does the term "God-breathed" mean to you?

When we hold the Word of God in our hands, we are holding the very words of the Holy Spirit, God's divine revelation of Himself to humanity. Gracious, that is miraculous, and yet I know how often I take it for granted.

For example, I'm prone to scroll social media more than I'm prone to scroll my Bible app. I search for inspirational words written by friends more than I search for the inspiration of the Holy Spirit through Scripture. I can justify this by telling you that most of whom I follow is for gospel-centered goodness. And that is true, except for when I'm searching for decorating inspiration, as you now know!

But there is only one way to become more of the Spirit-filled and Spirit-led mom that I long to be. Like we discovered yesterday, it is by letting the Word of God dwell in me richly. Not barely. *Richly*.

INSPIRED BY GOD

OPEN YOUR BIBLE and read 2 Timothy 3:16-17 (NIV).

> Notice how Paul opened this passage. How much of Scripture is God-breathed?

The word "all" reveals the danger in heeding the parts of the Bible we like and throwing out the parts we don't. If Paul taught that every last word is breathed out by God, what makes us believe we have the authority to discard what we disagree with or don't like?

What did Paul say Scripture is useful for?

What is the closing "so that" of this passage?

The Bible equips us with instruction, trains us in discipline, aligns our thoughts and actions with God's, and prepares us for the work God has planned for us. The Bible exists, at least in part, so that we may be complete—or know the salvation offered to us in Christ—and be equipped to walk out our salvation by doing the good work He planned for us.

Think specifically about your parenting for a moment. How dependent are you upon Scripture to be equipped for the work of God in your role as a mom?

What keeps you from dependency?

Eugene Peterson paraphrases 2 Timothy 3:16-17 beautifully in The Message paraphrase, affirming the inerrancy, essentiality, and sufficiency of Scripture:

> *Every part of Scripture is God-breathed and useful one way or another—showing us truth, exposing our rebellion, correcting our mistakes, training us to live God's way. Through the Word we are put together and shaped up for the tasks God has for us.*

Scripture shows us the truth that Jesus Christ did for us what we could never do for ourselves. The Holy Spirit melts our hearts with the grace of the gospel through Scripture. It is from this radical grace that we are open to having our rebellion exposed and our choices corrected. This radical grace breeds gratitude that makes us want to be trained to live God's way.

Through Scripture the Holy Spirit equips and shapes us "for the tasks God has for us," as Peterson helpfully puts it. Do we live like that's true, or do we mostly try to keep ourselves together and shape ourselves into the parents we long to be outside of Scripture?

OPEN YOUR BIBLE and read 2 Peter 1:20-21.

Who were the prophets "carried along by" (v. 21) as they spoke from God?

Just as a kite is carried along by the wind, and goes nowhere without the power and direction of the wind, so the prophets were wholly reliant on the power and direction of the Holy Spirit, who is symbolized by wind in Scripture (John 3:8).

To speak from God as they were "carried along by the Holy Spirit" means that the genuine words of the authors are also the genuine words of the Spirit.

"Prophecy is not a product of the prophet. Prophecy is a product of God through the Holy Spirit."[17]

In 2 Peter 1:21, Peter affirmed that Scripture was not conceived or created by man's imaginings, but rather, it was communicated through man under the inspiration of the Holy Spirit. God chose to involve people in the production of the Bible, but the Spirit is responsible for every word recorded in Scripture. This is how we can know that the Bible is the inerrant and sufficient Word of God: it's "God-breathed."

REVEALED BY THE SPIRIT

There's a profound connection between the Word and the Spirit in our lives. The Holy Spirit is not only the One who inspired Scripture but is also the One who illuminates the Word and helps us apply it.

Name three things the Holy Spirit does with Scripture, based on the statement above:

1.

2.

3.

The thing we often overlook about the Word is that the Spirit is always present, illuminating the words of Scripture and empowering us to apply it. We need the influence of the Spirit to experience the power of Scripture.

For example, I love gathering with and speaking to groups of women who have read my books or studies and want to have a conversation about what they read. I love knowing what's resonating and what's raising questions. Likewise, I know how much I love listening to other authors speak about the messages woven into their writing. Hearing directly from the author is special because you learn things you might have missed or overlooked in your reading. Or maybe you read something but didn't fully understand what the author intended to teach, but then you hear someone speak about it and there is a new depth to what you learned.

On a much grander scale, this is a lot like what the Holy Spirit does. He didn't just author the Bible; as we study God's Word, the Spirit speaks to us about it. There is no greater parenting book you will ever read than the Bible. And you have direct, unlimited access to the author Himself!

What are some of the topics that typically lead you to turn to parenting books or podcasts for help?

How likely are you to turn to Scripture about that topic as well? What is your hesitation, if any?

Obviously this isn't to say that we don't need to glean wisdom from parenting experts and those who have studied Scripture to help us be gospel-centered parents. The Holy Spirit is still very much in the business of speaking through people to help us grow in our understanding and relationship with God. But do we elevate talks and books above what the Holy Spirit wants to teach us or do in us directly through the Bible?

I know many mamas who say they lean toward books over the Bible because they don't feel equipped to unpack what they read or know how to teach it to their children. But this is even more motivation to welcome the Spirit into your study. "Holy Spirit, illuminate what you inspired" is a good prayer to start with.

OPEN YOUR BIBLE and read 1 John 2:27.

Mamas, a glorious part of our filling is the Holy Spirit clarifying and coaching us in what we read in Scripture. This anointing is so powerful, in fact, that John said we do not need anyone to teach us. This absolutely doesn't mean we shouldn't continually seek to glean wisdom from pastors and teachers or study the Bible in community with our sisters in Christ. It simply means don't neglect the Spirit in you who also wants to do this for you. This is an unbelievable benefit to having the Holy Spirit!

This also means you have what it takes to communicate truth to your children because the Holy Spirit in you enables you to teach them.

Moses commanded the Israelites in Deuteronomy 6:6-9 (NIV), and the same command applies to us today:

> *These commandments that I give you today are to be on your hearts.*
> *Impress them on your children. Talk about them when you sit at home and*
> *when you walk along the road, when you lie down and when you get up.*
> *Tie them as symbols on your hands and bind them on your foreheads.*
> *Write them on the doorframes of your houses and on your gates.*

Think of a time when something you read in Scripture specifically spoke to a struggle in your parenting. Explain how God worked in that situation.

LET HIM HELP YOU

If we want to better understand God's Word, we need the discernment of the Holy Spirit. For example, when we read Scripture and a verse jumps off the page at us—maybe even a verse we've read before but we now see something new in it—that's the Person of the Holy Spirit showing us exactly what He knows we need to read in that moment. It's why we can read the same verse a hundred times and have the Holy Spirit illuminate something new every time. God's Word is inexhaustible.

When we are comforted by Scripture, that's the Person of the Holy Spirit applying the living Word to our hurting hearts. When we are convicted by Scripture, that's the Person of the Holy Spirit—our Sanctifier—applying the living Word to our rebellious hearts. When we are strengthened by Scripture, that is the Holy Spirit—our Strengthener—applying the living Word to our feeble hearts.

> Reflect on the times when you experienced the Holy Spirit illuminating or applying Scripture in one of these ways. Record it here:

For the word of God is alive and powerful. It is sharper than the sharpest two-edged sword, cutting between soul and spirit, between joint and marrow. It exposes our innermost thoughts and desires.

HEBREWS 4:12, NLT

The word translated as "powerful" in this verse is the source of the word *energy*.[18] By this we know that the Spirit of the living God works in and through Scripture to expose what's below the surface. But it doesn't expose us to shame us. It exposes us to free us. It lays bare that which is in our hearts that isn't in alignment with God's righteous requirements. That is the work of the Spirit, through God's Word, so that we may know and have life to the fullest.

But we have to actually open, study, and marinate in the Word if we want Him to illuminate it. If we go to Scripture as a box to check rather than an opportunity for God to sharpen and refine us, we will miss out on what the Spirit wants to do in us and for us.

HOW DOES THIS EMPOWER MY PARENTING?

The extent to which we know God's Word and Spirit to be vital is the extent to which our relationship with Jesus will be vibrant. The Word is Christ, in an ultimate sense. The Bible centers on the Son (see Luke 24), and the ministry of the Spirit exalts the Son as we read the Bible. The Holy Spirit awakens us to the beauty of Jesus in the Word of God, and that is the most beautiful gift of all.

As mamas who long to display Christ to our children, let us approach Scripture with the same prayer as the psalmist, who wrote in Psalm 119:18 (NIV),

> *Open my eyes, that I may see wonderful things in your law.*

In that posture we welcome the Holy Spirit to illuminate the Words He alone inspired, and we can be sure He will show up to help us apply His instruction in our parenting and instill His Word in our children.

What an extraordinary gift the Holy Bible is. The Holy Spirit authored it, illuminates it, opens our hearts up to it, and empowers us to obey it.

DAY 3
HE GUIDES US IN TRUTH

I use Siri® to dictate almost every message I send. I much prefer dictation to typing. It's so habitual that when I recently left a friend a Voxer® message, I accidentally defaulted into dictating the message. I left her a message that sounded like this: "Hey, it's Jeannie period. Just wanted to let you know I'm thinking about you period. Let's catch up this week period. Call when you can exclamation point. Love you, friend smiley face." It wasn't until she messaged me back, telling me what a good laugh I'd given her in my dictating, that I realized what I'd done.

But here's the problem with dictating. Very often, Siri gets it wrong. Really wrong. If I don't check the dictation before I hit send (which is often the case when messaging with close friends), my message almost always has errors. Indeed, Siri can't always be trusted to communicate the truth on our behalf.

What does this have to do with the Holy Spirit? Let's get back to Bible study to see!

OPEN YOUR BIBLE and read John 16:13-15.

We are going to take these words of Jesus and break them down into four points to help us understand how the Spirit guides us in truth.

1. The Spirit points us to Jesus (v. 13).

Verse 13 says,

> *When the Spirit of truth comes, he will guide you into all the truth.*

Jesus called the Holy Spirit the Spirit of what?

Jesus assured the disciples that the Spirit would guide them into what?

The "all truth" Jesus spoke about is Himself. It's an understanding of the life, death, and resurrection of Jesus. It's every blessing and benefit bestowed on us in Jesus.

In reading that, your mind may be drifting to one of the most memorized verses in the Bible, where Jesus said, "I am the way, and the truth, and the life. No one comes to the Father except through me" (John 14:6). See the connection? The Spirit of truth guides us to the truth, Jesus Christ.

2. The Father sends the Spirit to speak truth to us (v. 13).

John 16:13 continues,

> For he will not speak on his own authority, but whatever he hears
> he will speak, and he will declare to you the things that are to come.

Whatever God wants to pass on to us is conveyed through His Spirit. And unlike Siri, He can always be trusted to say only the things God wants said. He never sends us the wrong message.

Think about Jesus' earthly ministry. While on earth, the Son never made a move without the leadership of His Father. Jesus Himself testified to this when He said,

> Very truly I tell you, the Son can do nothing by himself;
> he can do only what he sees his Father doing,
> because whatever the Father does the Son also does.
> JOHN 5:19, NIV

What does this verse tell us about the unity of the Trinity?

God the Son and God the Spirit are always speaking and working in ways that are consistent with their respective eternal relations with God the Father. Or, put another way, when God works, He works from the Father through the Son and in the Spirit. That is wild! God speaks to us. Directly. Personally. Specifically. The Spirit is the One who makes it possible, and He can always be trusted. May we never take this incredible benefit for granted. As Christians, our relationship with Jesus enables us to hear from the Holy Spirit.

What keeps you from expecting the Holy Spirit to speak to your spirit?

Of course this doesn't mean we should expect a loud, audible voice booming into our homes from heaven, helping us solve all of our parenting problems, although who am I to say how He might choose to speak to you. But most often it's by way of His Spirit speaking to our spirit.

I'll give you a recent example of how God answered my prayer very specifically.

I was driving alone and speaking with God, sharing my frustration that our boys have so few Christian friends in our community to grow and wrestle through their faith with. My heart was, and had been for a while, very heavy for my boys; it isn't easy following Jesus as a teen when you're doing it almost entirely alone. It's lonely and isolating. And to be totally honest, I was questioning God: *Why would You plant us where our boys can't have a strong faith community? Why wouldn't You provide for my kids in a way that seems so necessary to their faith? That doesn't seem like something a good Father would do.*

Soon thereafter, as I continued to drive, the words, *I don't have your family here to let your kids down,* came to mind and settled on my spirit, and I knew this message came from God. (How did I know? Because what was said aligns with what Scripture says about God's character and faithfulness. It sounded like the Spirit because it glorified Jesus.) That word spoken to my spirit offered a hopefulness that God knew I very much needed.

However, it was only weeks later when I was sitting in a worship service during a time of prayer, and once again deeply burdened by the fact that my boys don't have a strong community of faith, telling God that I still wasn't convinced He was at work in their hearts. (Mercy, He is so patient.) I wept real tears through the sermon because so much of what the pastor taught spoke to the doubt I'd just expressed to God. But it was the closing song that floored me with the repeated lyric, "You're never gonna let me down."

There He was, being so gentle with my doubt and speaking so clearly to my fear, assuring me again through the words, "I won't let you down," that He will be faithful to my family.

The Spirit speaks through Scripture, the words of a wise friend, a lyric of a song, a verse someone passes along, or straight to our spirit. Our job is to learn His voice so we know it's Him, and this happens by getting into God's Word, spending time with Him in prayer and conversation, and being tender to His presence.

Do you long to hear from God? Do you need Him to speak wisdom into the decisions in front of you? Maybe it's what course of treatment to choose for an illness, or what job to take, or which school to send your child to, or where to live, or how to have a hard conversation with a family member, or how to guide a rebellious child. Do you need His nudging to help you keep from sinning or to help you see opportunities where you can be a blessing? Maybe you need His voice of love to speak into the void in your heart. He is speaking. Are we listening?

> Where do you long to hear from Him today? Take time now to invite Him to speak into your circumstance.

3. The Spirit helps us glorify God (v. 14).

In the beginning of John 16:14, Jesus said, "He will glorify me."

> Whom will the Spirit glorify?

Being led by the Spirit is for any believer who will listen, and what He speaks will always glorify Jesus. This is the ultimate assurance that what we hear is the truth spoken by the Spirit.

We have studied the word *glorify* already, but let's review it briefly again. *Glorify* is the Greek word *doxazō*, which can be translated in a variety of ways depending on its context. It can be rendered "to extol, to praise, to magnify, to worship, to give honor, to give adulation, or to express one's fame or repute," and in this verse, it actually encompasses the full range of these meanings.[19] Shortly after Jesus explained that the Holy Spirit's goal is to glorify Him, He prayed,

> *Father, the hour has come; glorify your Son that the Son may glorify you.*
> JOHN 17:1

Jesus didn't seek glory apart from His Father's glory. We glorify the Father and Son in the power of the Holy Spirit, but the Spirit "with the Father and the Son is worshiped and glorified," as the Nicene Creed states.[20] He persuades us to pray that our lives would point to Jesus and not to ourselves. He makes much of Jesus in us and through us. If we want our lives to be signposts to the saving love of Jesus, we need to welcome the work of the Spirit of truth.

Look back at the full range of meanings of the word "glorify" in the text. Do any of those words represent how we approach our mothering? Explain.

We love our kids desperately, and we will do just about anything to do right by them. It's not wrong for us to want to be someone our kids can look up to; that's actually biblical. We want to be good role models whom our children can emulate. We want to demonstrate holy living that overflows from an obedient heart by the power of the Spirit. But it's easy to unknowingly step into wanting to be seen as perfect in their eyes rather than being willing to be seen as someone who must daily fall upon the grace of God—a grace that washes away our sin and shapes us into the likeness of our Savior.

A self-glorifying life is a certain sign that we lack the activity of the Holy Spirit. The Holy Spirit wants to free us of the pressure to be worthy of our kids' worship. He wants to change our desires from wanting to be worthy of worship to seeing our kids wanting to worship the only worthy One.

What is a specific way Jesus is glorified through your parenting?

The Spirit wants to glorify Jesus through our lives, and our parenting "perfection" isn't part of the equation. I'd go so far as to say that if we are forgiveness seekers and givers, pointing our kids to the grace and forgiveness we receive daily from Christ, then we have brought glory to God, just as the fruit we bear brings glory to Him.

4. The Spirit combats the lies of the enemy (vv. 14-15).

John 16:14-15 continues,

> For he will take what is mine and declare it to you. All that the Father has is mine; therefore I said that he will take what is mine and declare it to you.

The Spirit will declare the truth. His whole goal is glorifying Jesus and filling our minds with life-giving truth.

Now let's contrast this passage with what Jesus said about the devil just a few chapters earlier.

OPEN YOUR BIBLE and read John 8:44.

Record some of the stark differences between the Holy Spirit and the devil.

THE HOLY SPIRIT	THE DEVIL

We have an aggressive and persistent enemy who is committed to the polar opposite purpose of the Holy Spirit. He is the ultimate deceiver. I can only imagine the conviction with which Jesus spoke when He warned His disciples of the devil's deceit. I sense Jesus' holy anger over the father of lies.

Without the Spirit we stay entangled in the enemy's web of lies that keeps us from a free and flourishing life. This is why we need the Spirit of truth.

My dear friend Courtney is so good at calling out the enemy's lies in my life. We check in with each other almost daily, often via text, and whenever she reads a text from me that suggests insecurities are getting the best of me, or when I share painful narratives that are running through my head about my children, she doesn't hold back: "Jeannie, you know that is the devil. Those are straight-up lies!" Then she'll shoot off multiple texts full of truth. My phone will blow up with truth to replace the lie.

I believe this is what the Holy Spirit, our loyal friend, wants to do for us, but oh-so-much more. He wants to align the thoughts of our minds continually with the truth of God's Word.

> What specific lies do you struggle with regularly? Lies about unworthiness or insignificance? Lies about being invaluable or invisible? Lies about being an unqualified or unworthy mother? Lies about God not finishing what He started in your children. Name them here.

Based on what we've discovered so far, what steps can you take or practices can you put into place with the Spirit to help you silence the enemy?

OK, now check out how cool this is. Just a few verses earlier, in John 8:31-32,

Jesus said to the Jews who had believed him,
"If you abide in my word, you are truly my disciples,
and you will know the truth, and the truth will set you free."

Jesus promises us a freedom that cannot be found outside of Him alone, the truth Himself. Jesus sets us free with His sacrifice, and the Spirit guides us in the truth that freed us. The Spirit's goal is to guide us to the gospel—the good news that Jesus' perfect life, death, and resurrection have demonstrated God's unwavering love for us and secured His acceptance of us, delight in us, and pleasure over us.

Unlike our enemy, who relentlessly feeds us lies, the Holy Spirit frees our minds from all the lies we allow ourselves to believe! He guides our minds to the truth of who we are in Christ and makes it real to our hearts, empowering transformation at our very core.

HOW DOES THIS EMPOWER MY PARENTING?

Let us not forget this is what God delights to do in our children as well. It breaks our hearts to see our children believe the enemy's lies, but let us find great hope in the Holy Spirit who is fighting for their minds too!

What lies are your children believing that are breaking your heart?

What have you discovered today about the Spirit of truth that encourages you as a parent?

In closing today, take the lies your children are believing to the Lord and ask the Spirit of truth to invade their minds with the love of Christ and the assurance of their identity as His chosen children.

DAY 4
HE SPEAKS THROUGH ME

When we were walking through a very difficult season with one of our boys, I shared some of my heartbreak with one of my dear friends so she could be praying for him. I remember saying to her, "We have to get this right. We can't mess this up. If I don't say the right things to him, I could make this so much worse." My words held just the right amount of self-induced pressure and lack of trust in God's sovereignty that I was able to identify what I was doing. I was parenting in dependence on myself. I wanted to say it all right so my son would be all right. I was relying on my own wisdom (none of which I really had for this particular situation) while all along I had the Holy Spirit, who was ready to speak through me to my son.

Throughout Scripture we see a pattern of the Spirit speaking not just *to* people but *through* people, so we shouldn't be surprised that this is something He still does for us today. He speaks through us now if we let Him. This is the supernatural breaking into the natural in the most wonderful way.

HE SPEAKS TO AND THROUGH US
OPEN YOUR BIBLE and read Mark 13:11-13.

Can you imagine this moment? Jesus sat on the Mount of Olives, speaking privately with Peter, James, John, and Andrew about the signs of the end of the age. Jesus knew they would be accused on account of Him, would face severe persecution because of Him, and would need the supernatural help of the Holy Spirit to bear witness to Him.

> Do you believe not being anxious is possible for you to experience today? Why or why not? Or how do you experience this today?

Just as Jesus said the Spirit would give the disciples the words to say—so much so that it would actually be the Spirit speaking—so it is with us! This is one of the benefits that I cherish most as a mama.

The assurance for us is that if the Holy Spirit can help the disciples speak in such dire circumstances, how much more can we count on Him to speak to us and through us in our daily struggles and darkest battles. Hear Jesus saying to your heart even now, *Mama, don't be anxious, because My Spirit will give you the words to say.*

The Holy Spirit is a skilled communicator. He knows what to say when we are at a loss for words or need to speak into a difficult situation. He can help us articulate the feelings we can't make sense of or are too afraid to say. He knows what to pray when we don't know what we need or want. (We'll explore this benefit more in depth next week.)

> When have you found yourself in a difficult situation with your child and you desperately needed wisdom?

> Can you recall a time when you relied on the Holy Spirit to guide you in what to say? What happened?

"For it is not you who speak, but the Holy Spirit" (v. 11) is something I often encounter when I'm writing. I ask the Holy Spirit to speak to me when I study the Word of God and through me when I put my fingers on the keyboard. Then I count on Him to show up like He says He will. I used to feel arrogant saying that, like, who am I to suggest that God gives me what to say when I write about Him? It felt bold to suggest that my writing was guided by God. But that nonsense was replaced with the truth that this is a gift given to every believer. It doesn't make me special; it makes me His. God's Spirit inspires every human soul who puts his or her hope in Jesus—all for His glory.

THE SPIRIT'S WORDS

OPEN YOUR BIBLE and read 1 Corinthians 2:1-16.

Much like yesterday, we are going to break this passage down so we don't miss the many benefits of how He communicates through us.

1. Speak His words (vv. 3-5,13).

In 1 Corinthians 2:3-5,13 (NIV), Paul wrote:

> I came to you in weakness with great fear and trembling. My message and my preaching were not with wise and persuasive words, but with a demonstration of the Spirit's power, so that your faith might not rest on human wisdom, but on God's power. ... This is what we speak, not in words taught us by human wisdom but in words taught by the Spirit, explaining spiritual realities with Spirit-taught words.

In verse 4 Paul said his message was a demonstration of whose power?

What is the "so that" in verse 5?

How did Paul say he explained spiritual realities in verse 13?

If we want our lives to point our children to the power of God, we are encouraged to let our words be a demonstration of the Spirit's power. God wants us to speak with Spirit-taught words. This is an incredible benefit to having the Holy Spirit.

John Piper writes,

> "The words of Jesus have already been given to us. The four Gospels, formed out of Jesus's teachings, are a mountain of treasures. We are to listen to the words of Christ (Mark 9:7), and give them a home in our minds (John 8:37), and treasure them (Colossians 3:16). This is the raw material that the Holy Spirit works with as he teaches us what to say. He inspired the words of Jesus the first time. He loves to use them when the time comes."[21]

2. Identify His voice (vv. 11-12).

Now let's look at verses 11-12:

> For who knows a person's thoughts except their own spirit within them? In the same way no one knows the thoughts of God except the Spirit of God. What we have received is not the spirit of the world, but the Spirit who is from God, so that we may understand what God has freely given us.

What does verse 11 teach you about the Spirit's connection to the thoughts of God?

What does verse 12 teach you about what the Spirit wants to do for you?

Part of the Spirit's purpose within us is to help us think about things the way God thinks, to enable us to discern God's will for our lives, and to help us understand the things God has freely given us in His love.

But a question I know a lot of us ask is, *How do I know if it's actually the Holy Spirit wanting to communicate with me and through me or if it's just me convincing myself of something?*

A good starting place for answering that question is by asking these questions: *Does what I'm hearing or sensing align with the truth of Scripture? Does it align with the character of God? Does it glorify Jesus?*

When have you sensed something being spoken to your spirit that didn't meet these criteria? Explain.

One question that can be helpful in situations when you're trying to discern something you're feeling in your heart and mind is this: *Does this sound like the Advocate or the accuser (Rev. 12:10)?* (Remember that the Holy Spirit is called our Advocate!)

The Advocate will not speak with condemnation or accusation. He will not guide you outside of God's will. If the message you are hearing isn't rooted in love, you know who's speaking, and it's not the Holy Spirit. (This doesn't mean it will always feel good. Love and truth are how He communicates. The truth doesn't always feel good. But His voice won't carry shame. It will turn you toward repentance and refreshment, forgiveness and freedom.)

The Spirit gives grace. The devil heaps shame.
The Spirit advocates. The devil destroys.
The Spirit comforts. The devil disturbs.
The Spirit convicts. The devil condemns.
The Spirit keeps you free. The devil enslaves.

The Holy Spirit will never communicate anything that is not in alignment with God's Word, so we always need to test what we sense with what God's Word says. And this is why we need to be in our Bibles! We can't know the voice and character of God without the Word of God.

SPIRIT-EMPOWERED REMEMBRANCE
OPEN YOUR BIBLE and read John 14:26-27.

What two things did Jesus say the Helper would do for the disciples in verse 26?

When Jesus told His disciples that the Holy Spirit "will teach you everything and will remind you of everything I have told you" (John 14:26, NLT), He was instructing them on the coming ministry of the Spirit. At this point, the disciples didn't understand what was happening, but Jesus knew exactly what He was doing, and He was front-loading them for what would lie ahead.

This sounds a lot like our lives today, right? Jesus knows our tomorrows, but we often don't understand what's happening in our homes or in the lives of our kids.

"Jesus, I don't understand why you're allowing my child to go through this painful experience," or "Jesus, I don't see you at work in this struggle in my child's life" are things I've said on more than one occasion. I long to know what to do or what to say to speak into their pain and provide hope, but I also don't understand what Jesus is doing.

And while my desire to speak into my kids' lives is good and right, my worry reveals misplaced trust. I'm relying on my own understanding or banking on better circumstances rather than on the One who holds all things together in His faithful hands and will guide me in what to do and say when I am led by His Spirit.

Jesus was teaching them that the Spirit was going to help them recall everything they needed to remember. From Old Testament prophecy to the very words they witnessed spoken from the mouth of their Master, the Spirit would bring it to memory. The New Testament bears witness to the fulfillment of this promise, starting in the Book of Acts (for example, see Acts 2), where we see the disciples speaking and witnessing in the power of the Spirit over and over again.

Then Jesus offered the most tender word of comfort to His disciples. It's the same word of comfort I believe He wants to speak to us today.

Fill in your name on the line below and let the Lord speak His peace over your troubled heart and fearful thoughts.

"_____, Peace I leave with you; my peace I give to you. Not as the world gives do I give to you. Let not your hearts be troubled, neither let them be afraid."

In what areas do you need the peace of God to invade your parenting today? About what is your heart troubled or afraid?

When has the Holy Spirit brought to memory the truth of Scripture? What difference did that Scripture make in your situation?

I have a list formulating already. What Jesus said to the disciples is still true for us today. The Holy Spirit wants to speak to us and remind us of God's promises. This is where we find our peace. Not in better circumstances but in His promises!

Just like the Holy Spirit would help the disciples, He will help us recall what we have read and studied in Scripture. He will bring to memory what has already been stored. But He can't remind us of things we don't know. This is why we need to be steeped in the Word.

My daddy was an incredible preacher. The highest compliment I've ever received after speaking was from someone who had also heard my dad preach. She simply told me I teach just like my dad. I'm certain I didn't deserve such a compliment, but it makes sense, since I sat under his teaching for eighteen years before leaving for college. One of the things I loved most about my daddy's preaching was the way the very words of God were grafted into His sermons and how He would recite Scripture without needing to read it. Scripture was so woven into the fabric of his being that the Spirit could bring it to memory so easily. Daddy's memory has faded over recent years, and his mind is foggy, but do you know what hasn't faded? His ability to recall Scripture and teach truth. It astonishes me how sharp his mind remains around the things of God, and I believe it's because the Spirit still brings it to memory.

Scripture memory was an incredible gift my parents passed down to me, and it's a gift I long to pass down to my children. I didn't realize how valuable it was at the time, but I can think of few things I'm more grateful for than having a storehouse of Scripture for the Spirit to work with.

> If Scripture memory is something you practice in your home, take a moment to write down what's been helpful in your home that you can share with others who want to learn this practice.

> What is one step you can take this week to prioritize Scripture memory with your kids?

HE SPEAKS THROUGH OTHER BELIEVERS

I was recently driving in the car with a very Spirit-filled friend, and I was sharing some of the struggles Mike and I were facing in our marriage. But instead of responding with advice or ideas, she began to speak with such power and boldness and truth that I knew it was the Holy Spirit speaking to me. He was speaking through my friend what He wanted to say to me. And let me assure you, most of what she had to say wasn't easy to hear, but it was necessary. It was love *and* truth. Then she put her hand on me and began to pray for our marriage and for breakthrough in the pattern of unhelpful communication that we were stuck in. The Holy Spirit's presence was palpable in my car.

Goodness let's surround ourselves with friends like that!

How did I know it was from the Holy Spirit? The message aligned with the Word of God, it aligned with the character of God, and it glorified Jesus. I also felt the Spirit's presence and loving conviction as she spoke.

> Have you been the recipient of the Holy Spirit speaking to you through someone else? Or did the Holy Spirit give you a word of truth to share with your child or someone you love? Explain.

HOW DOES THIS EMPOWER MY PARENTING?

Are you struggling with how to communicate with your child? Are you desperate for wisdom to speak into your child's life? Are you longing to lead your child to the truth of who Jesus is?

The Holy Spirit wants to speak through you to lead your children in truth. Do you believe He can? Do you believe He will? Have an honest conversation with Him about your hopes, your fears, your doubts. Welcome Him to show His power in your speech. Welcome Him to invade your heart and mind with His wisdom and to empower you to speak it over your children!

#NeverAloneBibleStudy

THE CHAMPIONING OF THE HOLY SPIRIT

Do you have a friend, or maybe it's your spouse, who you know is undoubtedly for you? Someone who always has your back, someone who not only cheers for you but will hold up your arms when you feel weak? Someone who can just sense when something is wrong and is willing to sit with you in the pain but also speaks life-giving truth over you so you don't get stuck there? Someone who is genuinely excited to see you use your God-given gifts and watch your God-given dreams come to fruition? This kind of friend is more precious than gold.

Likewise, I bet we'd say we do this for our children. We champion them. We are for them in every imaginable sense. There isn't anything we wouldn't do to help them know the love of Jesus, to reorient their hearts away from their rebellious ways and toward their resurrected Savior. We speak life and hope into their heartaches. We pray down the power of heaven to move in their hearts and do what only He can do in their lives.

Isn't it wild to know that the Holy Spirit does this for us? We might oftentimes be unaware of it, just as our children are oftentimes unaware of everything we're doing behind the scenes to spur them on, but it remains true. The eternal God Himself champions us. A *champion* is "an ardent supporter or defender."[22] A person who fights or argues for a cause on behalf of someone else. Supporter, protector, defender, promoter. A battler on your behalf. Oh yes, I need this Person of the Holy Spirit in my life today and every day. He champions us by infusing intimacy into our relationship with God, giving us hope when circumstances in our children's lives feel hopeless, praying for us and our children for things we don't even know to ask for, growing us and our children in the likeness of Jesus, and so much more.

Sister, I'm so excited for us to discover how the Spirit champions us and our children for the glory of the Father this week!

DAY 1
HE BRINGS INTIMACY WITH GOD

OPEN YOUR BIBLE and read Romans 8:12-28.

Now let's focus on verses 14-17 together.

> *For all who are led by the Spirit of God are sons of God. For you did not receive the spirit of slavery to fall back into fear, but you have received the Spirit of adoption as sons, by whom we cry, "Abba! Father!" The Spirit himself bears witness with our spirit that we are children of God, and if children, then heirs—heirs of God and fellow heirs with Christ, provided we suffer with him in order that we may also be glorified with him.*

Paul affirmed that when we are sons or daughters of God, we get to be led by the Spirit of God. Notice I said "get to." This is so different than "have to" or even "should be." We *get to* be led by Almighty God in our daily lives. Do we know what an incredible benefit this is to having the indwelling Holy Spirit?

In verse 15, Paul contrasted the spirit of _____ with the Spirit of _____.

What did Paul say the spirit of slavery causes us to do?

What did Paul say the Spirit of adoption causes us to do?

ADOPTED BY GOD
Our family recently returned from our fourth annual trip to Danita's Children's Home in Haiti. This is a loving Christian home where about one hundred children, who have been orphaned, are being raised and nurtured. This is also where our son Andre grew up.

Each year that we travel to Danita's, our relationships with the children deepen, and the children grow more open in sharing their stories with us, allowing us to enter into the pain they've experienced from the death or abandonment of their parents. They have endured things no child should ever have to walk through. But there is a deep gratitude in my heart for how God has used Danita's to help the children grow in the knowledge of their adoption as beloved children of God.

Abba is the Aramaic word Jesus used for Father in the Lord's prayer. *Abba* "can either be understood as 'the father' or the more personal, 'my father.'"[23]

I don't think you have to be an orphan to grasp the magnitude of your adoption as children of God, but I can tell you this: There is no place on earth where I have experienced how "the Spirit himself bears witness with our spirit that we are children of God, and if children, then heirs—heirs of God and fellow heirs with Christ," as Paul wrote in Romans 8:16-17, like I do when I'm with the children at Danita's. They hold sacred the invitation to cry out "Abba! Father!" and they do it with such a contagious thirst to know Him. I have experienced some of my most intimate moments with Jesus on Danita's campus.

But something else really beautiful happened on our last trip. Karris, one of the missionaries who has been an incredible mom to these children over the last twenty years, expressed feeling many of the same struggles that any one of us experience as moms. The enemy tempts her to worry that she isn't enough or isn't doing enough when it comes to walking with her kids through their worries, fears, hardships, or dreams. But she also shared with me how she is learning afresh how to be led by the Spirit as she parents the children. She is learning to lean into His voice about when to speak into a situation or when to stay silent and trust His conviction in her kids' lives. She is learning to trust the Holy Spirit to hold them close when she can't. She is learning to be led by the Spirit of adoption rather than the spirit of slavery to fear. And it's bringing her immense freedom from the pressure to be who only the Father can be to her kids.

What does it mean for you as a mom to be led by the Spirit of adoption rather than the spirit of slavery to fear?

When have you experienced the Spirit bearing witness with your spirit that you are a child of God (Rom. 8:16), giving you the priceless assurance of who you are and what is yours in Christ?

The Message so beautifully paraphrases Romans 8:15-17 like this:

> *This resurrection life you received from God is not a timid, grave-tending life. It's adventurously expectant, greeting God with a childlike "What's next, Papa?" God's Spirit touches our spirits and confirms who we really are. We know who he is, and we know who we are: Father and children. And we know we are going to get what's coming to us—an unbelievable inheritance! We go through exactly what Christ goes through. If we go through the hard times with him, then we're certainly going to go through the good times with him!*

The Spirit of adoption champions us by confirming in our spirit who we really are—children adopted by a loving Father into an unbelievable, eternal inheritance of an eternity in the presence of God where there is freedom from the brokenness of this world. We won't walk through anything Christ didn't endure before us, but more than that, we will also share in Christ's inheritance and ultimately glorification—when we share in God's glory—with Him. This world is not our home—our home is the paradise God has prepared for us. Until then we have the Holy Spirit to remind us of what's to come.

OUR ETERNAL INHERITANCE

Our adoption as God's children means we also share in the inheritance. This adoption means we're welcome to call God Abba, Father—to call God our Father with assurance and boldness.

Paul spoke to this intimate relationship again in Galatians 4:6-7 (MSG):

> *You can tell for sure that you are now fully adopted as his own children because God sent the Spirit of his Son into our lives crying out, "Papa! Father!" Doesn't that privilege of intimate conversation with God make it plain that you are not a slave, but a child? And if you are a child, you're also an heir, with complete access to the inheritance.*

One of the ways the Spirit champions us is to make God's love grow from awareness in our head to affection in our heart. He stirs our hearts to call out to Him as Abba, Father, and He welcomes us into the intimacy of the Trinity that we were made to enjoy.

> Does God's love fall more into the category of "knowledge in your head" or "affection in your heart?" Or both? Based on the passages we've read, what is the Spirit's role in making His love grow to affection in your heart?

Tim Keller writes beautifully about this benefit:

> *"When the Holy Spirit comes down on you in fullness, you can sense your Father's arms beneath you. It is an assurance of who you are. The Spirit enables you to say to yourself: 'If someone as all-powerful as that loves me like this, delights in me, has gone to infinite lengths to save me, says he will never let me go, and is going to glorify me and make me perfect and take everything bad out of my life—if all of that is true—why am I worried about anything?' At a minimum this means joy, and a lack of fear and self-consciousness."* [24]

> Does the idea of intimacy with the Trinity seem foreign or even unattainable to you? Or is it familiar and irresistible? Explain.

An intimate relationship with God is central to our ability to parent in the power of the Spirit. If we want to be led by the Spirit as we lead our children, we need to know His heart, His voice, and His ways. Close, rich fellowship with God is one of the most treasured gifts the Holy Spirit gives us, so if intimacy feels foreign or uncomfortable to you, would you dare to ask the Spirit to pry your heart open to the great flood of assurance He wants to pour in?

Of course, we know intimacy requires vulnerability. We can't have an intimate relationship with someone we aren't willing to be unguarded with. This means that to enjoy an intimate relationship with God, we are going to need to be open to and unresistant with the Spirit. We'll need to trust Him and be trusting of what He's been given to do in our lives.

But this needn't be difficult to do because of how very trustworthy the Spirit has proven to be. There is none more worthy of our trust than our triune God!

OPEN YOUR BIBLE and read Philippians 3:3.

According to the apostle Paul, how do we worship?

Our worship is empowered by the Spirit. It's the Holy Spirit who gives us the desire to marinate in the Lord's love. He stirs us to stand and celebrate and rejoice in God's splendor. He woos us to sit quietly and savor God's tender presence. The Holy Spirit shines the spotlight on Christ's sacrifice and shows us there's nothing better than being called God's son or daughter.

GUARD AGAINST THE ENEMY

Of all the things the enemy does not want you to experience, I believe intimacy with God through the Holy Spirit is at the top of the list. The enemy knows he's done for once you resonate with what the psalmist said: "Better is one day in your courts than a thousand elsewhere" (Ps. 84:10, NIV). The Holy Spirit shows us there is no substitute for being in God's presence and no greater joy found outside of it. To feel truly known by God and to experience the warmth of His presence and His welcoming acceptance is better than the best this world can offer, and the enemy knows that. But we will "not be outwitted by Satan; for we are not ignorant of his designs" (2 Cor. 2:11).

Have you considered why the enemy would want you to keep the Spirit at arm's length? How does today's study inspire you to welcome the confidence He wants to give you as God's beloved, and the affection He wants to stir in your spirit for Jesus?

When life feels like it's going off the rails. When illness strikes. When your marriage is struggling. When you ache over choices your kids are making or rejection they're facing or internal battles that are waging, the Spirit stirs us to cry out "Abba! Father!" To run to the Father as our safe harbor and sure foundation.

> Is there anything you want to run to Him with now? Pause here and take a moment to do that.

HOW DOES THIS EMPOWER MY PARENTING?
God longs for a loving and intimate relationship with His children. We worship a God who is both omnipotent and intimate. This perfect love beckons us to call the Alpha and Omega our Abba, Father. The One who holds all things together also holds us together. He holds our children together. He holds our homes together.

That being said, I realize that the idea of intimacy with God can make some feel uncomfortable, especially if they were raised in a home where God was seen as a distant Being rather than as a relational Father. And this can often impact how we, in turn, teach our kids about God.

> How has your experience as a child impacted your parenting and how you speak with and teach your children about God?

> What are you learning about the Spirit's essential role in knowing God as a relational and trustworthy Father?

Join me in closing and ask the Spirit to stir up the assurance of our adoption as we sit in the presence of our Abba, Father, that we might be empowered to teach and model this priceless intimacy to our children.

DAY 2
HE MAKES US ABOUND IN HOPE

Have you ever been afraid to hope? Maybe something you've suffered has been so painful that you couldn't fathom anything good on the other side of it. Or maybe something your children have chosen to do or pursue was so inconsistent with who God has made them to be that it has felt foolish to keep the hope for them, like you were just setting yourself up for disappointment. Or maybe you've been praying for breakthrough in a situation that remains unchanged, so you've given up hoping things can ever look differently. Or maybe it feels like you're literally drowning in dirty laundry and disciplining kids and dying dreams, and hope feels lost on you.

I recognize how hard it can be to maintain hope, especially in today's world. That's why I'm so grateful today's study of Romans 8 reveals the Spirit's vital role in helping us abound in hope.

Today we will pick up in verse 18, where Paul wrote about suffering and hope and future glory.

ALREADY AND NOT YET
OPEN YOUR BIBLE and read Romans 8:18-25.

In this passage, Paul described the tension of the already and not yet—how we live as followers of Christ in a broken world while we wait for Jesus to return.

> Look closely at verses 22-23 and note how Paul compared groaning from the pain of childbirth to how creation groans for the not yet. When do you feel that groan? That angst that makes us cry out, "How long, Lord?" Explain.

What is this thing Paul mentioned in verse 23 about us having "the firstfruits of the Spirit" while we wait for the not yet? The firstfruits of the Spirit mean we have received only a taste of what is to come. It's really a pledge that so much more is awaiting us. The Spirit gives us a taste of the full freedom that is to come: the glory that awaits us when God will restore our souls, we will receive our new resurrection bodies, and the entire cosmos will be renovated. But waiting for this requires great patience, which is thankfully not something we have to muster up, but rather, is a fruit that the Spirit manifests in us (Gal. 5:22-23).

What about the previous paragraph stands out to you the most? Why?

We are already adopted but we hope for the fullness of our freedom—freedom from the effects of sin and death. Our hope isn't just what gets us through the struggles and the pain. There's more to it than that.

HOLD ONTO HOPE
Let's look at what Paul wrote about hope a few chapters earlier in Romans 5:3-5:

We rejoice in our sufferings, knowing that suffering produces endurance, and endurance produces character, and character produces hope, and hope does not put us to shame, because God's love has been poured into our hearts through the Holy Spirit who has been given to us.

What does suffering produce?

What does endurance produce?

What does character produce?

What did Paul say hope does not do in verse 5?

How is God's love poured into our hearts?

Can you identify a time when you witnessed this to be true in something your kids walked through? A team they didn't make, a friend who turned their back, a learning disability, persistent anxiety, an illness or injury, depression, feeling unworthy, or rejection from the school they hoped to attend.

Just days ago I was able to witness the truth of this passage worked out in one of my sons, who shared how God's love is becoming more real to him after having walked through a pretty difficult season. It's incredibly difficult to watch our kids struggle and suffer, isn't it? In fact, I can't think of anything more painful. But since we know this is a normal part of life on this side of heaven, it's encouraging to remember that trials can confirm for our kids how confident hope in God's love is what carries us through suffering and is produced in greater measure because of it.

Experiencing the love of God is the sovereign and supernatural work of the Spirit of God. John Piper writes,

> *"He is an illuminator of the glory of God's love in the work of Christ. He is a heart-eye opener to the ravishing reality that in the death of Christ for us, God loved us infinitely."*[25]

Share a time when you sensed God's love and comfort during suffering or sadness. How did you know this was the supernatural work of the Holy Spirit?

"It is sobering that trusting in Christ brings sufferings. But it is satisfying that those sufferings produce endurance, which produces proven character, which produces a confident hope in God's enduring yet eternal care. God's Spirit gives God's love in abundance. This is the normal yet glorious life of gospel faith."[26]

I remember the loneliness I felt during my first semester at Auburn University. I loved everything about Auburn and the friends I was meeting, but I was also terribly homesick in those early days. I would call home every single morning from the landline in our dorm room (remember those?) and ask my parents to pray with me. It was how I got through the day.

On one particular morning that is impossible to forget, when it felt like the sadness would swallow me whole, my Dad prayed that I would know the comfort and presence of God in an overwhelming way that day. I was sitting on top of my dresser (not sure why I was up there) as my Dad prayed, and I felt what can only be described as a hug from God. I felt the undeniable comfort of His presence envelop me. It was the Holy Spirit making me aware of God's nearness in my loneliness. It was the comfort I craved that only He could provide.

My word of encouragement to mamas of older kids is let us not forget the power of our prayers and the Spirit's presence indwelling them even when we cannot be physically present with them. Loosening our grip and letting them fly is scary. But God their Father goes with them. If they are believers, His Spirit indwells them. They may not always yield to His authority in their lives, just like we don't always yield to the Spirit's authority in ours, but He will not give up on them or abandon them. His loving conviction will continue.

And if our older children are not believers, let us find great hope in the assurance that the Holy Spirit longs to reveal the beauty of Christ to our children even more than we long for them to receive Him. Let us continue to pray that their hearts would be opened to God's love in Jesus Christ through the power of the Holy Spirit.

Another deeply painful time in my life was when I had a miscarriage. We prayed so hard for that baby whose heart had just begun to beat when we were told it was unlikely he would survive based on his size. There were many weeks of waiting and begging God for a miracle, but a sonogram revealed there was no longer a heartbeat, and it was crushing. But this I can honestly say: the Holy Spirit's comfort enveloped me as I said goodbye to the baby I won't hold until heaven. I felt the warmth of His presence in that cold, sterile hospital room, assuring me I was not alone or without hope.

His comfort is the assurance that Jesus intimately knows our pain and won't waste our suffering.

Why does it matter that Jesus intimately knows our pain and suffering? What does it mean that Jesus won't waste our pain and suffering?

Paul wrote in 2 Corinthians 1:3-5:

> *Blessed be the God and Father of our Lord Jesus Christ,*
> *the Father of mercies and God of all comfort, who comforts*
> *us in all our affliction, so that we may be able to comfort those*
> *who are in any affliction, with the comfort with which we ourselves*
> *are comforted by God. For as we share abundantly in Christ's*
> *sufferings, so through Christ we share abundantly in comfort too.*

What would you add, if anything, to your answers on the previous page, based on 2 Corinthians 1:3-5?

WHAT IS BIBLICAL HOPE?
OPEN YOUR BIBLE and read Romans 15:4.

When Paul addressed the "former days" he was referring to the Old Testament. Paul taught here that the entirety of Scripture is given so that we might have hope!

Now skip down to verse 13 and write it below.

One way I experience the infilling of hope when my heart is sad or heavy is through reciting Psalm 42:5: "Why, my soul, are you downcast? Why so disturbed within me? Put your hope in God, for I will yet praise him, my Savior and my God." When I recite this psalm I tell my soul what to do. Declarations using the Word of God hold power. And the Spirit applies the hope!

Biblical hope is different from the kind of hope that relies on circumstances aligning to our liking. Even when our situation makes no sense to our finite minds, we can bank on God's unchanging love.

Through the power of the Holy Spirit we can have more than just a hopeful outlook in our suffering: By the power of Holy Spirit we can "abound in hope" (Rom. 15:13). This is His good work in us, especially when our grief or distress is rooted in what we can't control or fix in our kids' lives. Or when we feel so alone in our suffering and uncertain in our decision-making.

> "Biblical hope not only desires something good for the future —it expects it to happen. ... Biblical hope is not a mere desire for something good to happen. It is a confident expectation and desire for something good in the future. Biblical hope has moral certainty in it. When the word says, 'Hope in God!' it does not mean, 'Cross your fingers.' It means, to use the words of William Carey, 'Expect great things from God.'"[27]

Where are you expecting great things from God right now?

HOW DOES THIS EMPOWER MY PARENTING?

When I feel hopeless over things I see happening in our home or in my kids' lives, I have trusted friends I know I can call to ask for prayer or who will provide a word of encouragement. I know I can count on these friends to remind me of what's true about our God of hope and His promises. I can count on them to remind me what is true about my incredible kids. And while it's right and good to rely on our community of fellow believers when we are suffering or sad, let us not neglect the Holy Spirit, the One who is able to supernaturally fill us with hope. I want to encourage us not to forfeit this benefit of having the Holy Spirit who has been given to us to make us abound in hope.

> What do you tend to do with hopelessness? How do you handle it? Do you go to a friend? Your spouse? The Internet? A trusted Bible teacher? The Word?

Like Abraham, we are invited to live "fully convinced that God [is] able to do what he [has] promised" (Rom. 4:21). God can take what the enemy meant for our harm and use it for our good (Gen. 50:20).

Why are we never without hope? Because we are never without the Holy Spirit. Allow your troubles to rest in that knowledge today, Mama.

Let's invite our heavenly Father to breathe supernatural hope into the most delicate places of our hearts through the Holy Spirit.

Will you pray the passage we just read with me? *God of hope, fill me with all joy and peace in believing, so that by the power of Your Holy Spirit, I may abound in hope.*

DAY 3

HE HELPS US IN WEAKNESS

I remember a season when I was so exhausted and overwhelmed that I couldn't even mutter my prayers aloud, and I fell asleep every time I attempted to pray in silence. I was nursing a newborn who didn't sleep while also trying to parent our three older boys who were eight, ten, and twelve. But still, on Sunday mornings we somehow wrangled our whole crew into the car and made our way to church, because I desperately needed to be in an atmosphere of worship and allow hope to rise in my soul.

One Sunday, when I must have been looking especially wrecked, I ran into a friend who serves on the prayer team on the way out the door, and she asked if she could come by the house and pray for me. Tears filled my eyes, and she knew that my tears were saying, "Yes, please, yes" before I even spoke a word.

The following Tuesday she stopped by the house. When she asked me if there was anything specific she could pray for, the floodgates opened. I struggled to speak through my sobbing, "I don't even know. Anything!"

"It's OK, the Holy Spirit knows what you need," she assured me, and she began to pray.

My friend welcomed the Holy Spirit's prayers on my behalf, and I settled into the hope and strength of God that filled me in that hour. While I didn't turn into supermom, I did have a renewed sense of provision that I knew was from the Holy Spirit, and that was more than enough to carry me through those sleepless days.

What my friend demonstrated that day was the biblical truth that one way the Holy Spirit champions us is by helping us in our weakness.

HE STRENGTHENS ME

One of the greatest things about knowing the grace of God is the freedom to admit we are weak. There is so much pressure in our culture to pretend we are strong enough, in and of ourselves, to face what this life throws our way. But as Christians we enjoy the benefit of having the strength of the Spirit.

OPEN YOUR BIBLE and read 2 Corinthians 12:1-10.

Look specifically at verses 8-10. Paul taught that when we confess we are weak in the flesh, we are made strong in the Spirit. It sounds great, but how does it play out? Do we get zapped with strength when we confess we are weak? Of course not. So how is it that His power is made perfect in our weakness?

His power becomes real when we confess we have weaknesses that stand in the way of us becoming who we want to be or doing what we want to do. It is then that our weaknesses give way to God's strength. When we are busy pretending we don't have weaknesses, we miss out on experiencing God's supernatural strength.

When we trust the full sufficiency of God's strength, we are free to be honest about our weakness because then the pressure to pretend we are something we aren't is lifted, and the humility required to invite the power of the Spirit of God becomes undeniably precious to us.

It's easy to wish God would just remove weakness from us. But what God does for us is so much better than that. He gives us His Spirit, and He allows us to experience what's only possible with Him through our weakness. Paul was basically saying, "Because I'm good with having weaknesses, I get to experience Christ's power working through me." Christ's power is the Holy Spirit.

> How does this dialogue between God and Paul change how
> you view your weaknesses?

I was not OK with having weaknesses when I didn't understand the magnitude of God's grace. I was ashamed of my weakness. Embarrassed by my weaknesses, especially with my kids. I wanted them to see me as someone who would never let them down or get it wrong.

But now I have so much freedom to confess to my kids how much I need Christ's power to help me. I get to shine the spotlight on the perfection of Christ and His power that manifests in my life when I'm not afraid to admit I need His help. My weakness give evidence to God's power. Maybe it even makes my kids hungry to have His power—which is the Person of the Holy Spirit—too! And isn't that what we want for our kids? For them to know God's power in their lives?

Another benefit of being honest about our weakness is that it gives our kids permission to be honest about theirs. Kids mostly hide their struggles and shortcomings for fear of disappointing us or appearing inadequate, when what we really want is to be a safe place for them to speak openly about their struggles. When we're honest with our kids about our weakness, it opens up dialogue with our kids to freely share their own.

Identify weaknesses where you need to experience the Spirit's power in your parenting currently.

What is one step you can take today to be more intentional in welcoming the Spirit to strengthen you in your weakness?

When you find yourself in situations where you're saying, "I can't do this. I don't have what it takes. I don't have the courage. I don't have the energy. I don't have the strength," take heart and hear the Holy Spirit saying, "I can! I do!!" Take the help and then boast all the more that you don't have what it takes because *you* have the power of God living inside you, and He can do abundantly more! He will strengthen your heart for the work of your hands. He will strengthen you with power through his Spirit in your inner being (Eph. 3:16).

HE PRAYS FOR ME

Let's return now to Romans 8, picking back up at verse 26, to discover more of how the Holy Spirit helps us in weakness.

OPEN YOUR BIBLE and read Romans 8:26-29.

The Spirit "helps us in our weakness" and "intercedes for us" to the Father (v. 26). Did you know these were some of the benefits of having the Holy Spirit's indwelling presence? Maybe you knew this but how His help plays out has felt confusing or inaccessible. Good news, Mama! How He does this will be the topic of our study today, and I'm so excited about it.

When we don't know what to pray, the Holy Spirit prays for us with "groans" (v. 26). If you'll recall from our reading yesterday, the Holy Spirit isn't the only one who groans. We, too, groan inwardly.

How does the Holy Spirit groan for us? Timothy Keller writes,

> "Most of the time, we don't know exactly what outcome we should pray for. The Spirit, however, makes our groaning His groaning, putting His prayers to the Father inside our prayers. He does so by placing within us a deep, inexpressible longing to do God's will and see His glory. This aspiration—this 'groaning' desire to please Him—comes through in our petitions to God. In every specific request, then, the Father hears us praying for what is both truly best for us, and pleasing to Him, and the intercession of the Spirit is answered as God works all things for our good."[28]

The Father hears us praying through the intercession of the Holy Spirit. How does this make you think differently about what we tend to call "unanswered prayer"?

What are some unanswered prayers you have been praying for your child(ren)? What comfort can you take in knowing how the Holy Spirit is interceding for you and your children in these areas?

Take courage, my friend, because the Holy Spirit prays on your behalf. The needs nestled in our hearts that we don't know how to—or just can't—articulate become His cry on our behalf.

What joy should fill our souls when we sit in the assurance that the Holy Spirit's appeal on our behalf is very personal! He knows our frustrations, and He knows our longings. He knows we need help praying in accordance with God's will and discerning God's ways. So He takes the cries of our hearts—our groans—and goes to God on our behalf. As the Holy Spirit groans for you in perfect accordance with God's will, God discerns His wordless prayers perfectly.

So Jesus, who sits at the right hand of God Almighty, and the Holy Spirit, who dwells within you, are interceding for you. Look what we've been given. Look who we have in our corner!

Paul concluded with confidence,

> And we know that in all things God works for the good of those
> who love him, who have been called according to his purpose.
> ROMANS 8:28, NIV

I've heard it taught that the "good" is something like a better car if yours gets hit, or a better job if you get fired, or a better life if yours falls apart. And while all of these good things might actually be the outcome of bad things happening, the promise here is not earthly pleasures but something far more glorious.

Paul gave us the answer:

> For those God foreknew he also predestined to be conformed to the image
> of his Son, that he might be the firstborn among many brothers and sisters.
> ROMANS 8:29, NIV

Even through the Spirit's prayers for us, His sanctifying power is at work, because the way God works all things for our good is by conforming us "to the image of his Son" (v. 29). Isn't this the greatest desire of our hearts? For our lives to look more like our Savior's, full of the fruit of the Spirit? What an incredible promise.

Can you identify a time when God used a difficult situation in your
child's life to draw your child closer to Him? Or if your child is too
young to witness this, can you identify a time in your own life when this
has been true?

The Spirit's prayer is that whatever we endure would draw us closer to Jesus, make us more like Him, and produce His character in our lives. And this is true for our children. Whatever our children must endure (all of those things we cannot control or fix) can be used by their heavenly Father to draw them closer to His heart and conform them more into the likeness of Jesus. *Let it be so, Lord!* Isn't it just extraordinary to think that we get to partner with the Holy Spirit in the work He wants to do in our kids through our prayers?

Maybe your prayer life is on fire right now. Or maybe you're feeling a little bit like I did on the day my friend came over to pray for me. Or perhaps you have a heavy heart over decisions you have to make and you're afraid to pray for the wrong thing. Or maybe you worry about whether you're doing it right or saying it right, which makes prayer feel more like a laborious task than a glorious gift.

Paul has even more encouragement for us about this.

OPEN YOUR BIBLE and read Ephesians 6:10-20.

This is Paul's well-known teaching on putting on the whole armor of God. He warned we are in a spiritual battle against the enemy's lies and accusations, and he admonished us to "be strong in the Lord and in the strength of his might" (v. 10). We will get more into the strength we have in the Lord tomorrow, but for now I want us to notice Paul's instruction to take the "sword of the Spirit, which is the Word of God, praying at all times in the Spirit" (vv. 17-18).

Paul taught us to pray in the Spirit using the sword of the Spirit—the Bible. We pray in accordance with the Spirit when we pray the Spirit-inspired Word. We pray for our lives so that we have the armor of God, but praying Scripture for our kids is so incredibly powerful, Mama.

> If this is a practice you've incorporated into your parenting, what are some of the situations when you've witnessed the profound difference it makes in your kids' lives? ("Remembering" is an important practice. We can be quick to forget how God's worked in the past, but this practice spurs us on in the present!)

Let's practice this now. Insert your child's name into the verses below and make it your prayer for him/her today.

- Father, cause _____ to put her/his trust in You and never be shaken (Ps. 125:1).
- Father, let nothing unwholesome be on _____'s devices but only that which is helpful for building others up according to their needs (Eph. 4:29).
- Father, fill _____ with the knowledge of Your will through all spiritual wisdom and understanding, that he/she may live a life worthy of You and please You in every way (Col. 1:9-10).
- Father, equip _____ to flee from sexuality immorality, recognizing that his/her body is the temple of the Holy Spirit. Remind her/him that she/he belongs to You and she/he is to honor You with her/his body (1 Cor. 6:12-20).
- Father, when _____ wrestles with loneliness and rejection, remind him/her of Your promise: "For the mountains may depart and the hills be removed, but my steadfast love shall not depart from you, and my covenant of peace shall not be removed" from his/her life (Isa. 54:10).

Are there other verses you pray for your kids that have been powerful in your parenting? Record them here to share with others, if you're studying with a group.

HOW DOES THIS EMPOWER MY PARENTING?

Mike and I have been blown away at how God has specifically responded to our prayers through Scripture. The above verses were extracted from a book my friend Jodie Berndt wrote called, *Praying the Scriptures for Your Teens.*[29] My copy of Jodie's book is torn and tattered from my years of using it to guide my prayers for my children.

Jodie is a dear friend of mine, and on one particular day when I was sharing with her about a pattern of dishonesty in one of my boys, Jodie encouraged us to pray that the Spirit would expose the sin and folly in our kids' lives. Of course we pray that they would not fall to temptation and would always make wise and godly choices, but since we're not raising Jesus, we also need to pray that when their battle with the flesh wins, it doesn't stay hidden.

It's wild how God has answered this prayer and not allowed our kids to go too far down the wrong path in certain situations before helping us discover their folly. (Of course, I know we don't know about every time they've stumbled, but God has been faithful to expose sin in situations where Mike and I were able to speak into their struggles and decisions, to discipline and give consequences, to extend grace and forgiveness, and to give them a safe place to talk so shame doesn't fester in the secret places.)

Praying this way for our boys reminds me of a story from my childhood. When I was only eight I met my friend Morella in Sunday School at church, and she is still my dearest friend to this day. Morella's mom was one of the most Spirit-filled and Spirit-led women you'll ever meet. She was a second mom to me, and I loved her deeply. She is now with Jesus after a battle with cancer but this I will tell you: the older Morella and I got, the less I wanted to make poor choices when I was with Morella because her mom seemed to always have a sense of our sin. I didn't understand how she could know what she knew because this was long before things like Life360® and cell phones that can be searched by parents. But now I know. She was led by the Spirit. She prayed fervently for us, and her heart was tender to the Spirit's voice. Now that I'm a mom, I pray what Morella's mom prayed: *Lord, please reveal their sin so I can lead them to Your grace.*

I love knowing that the Holy Spirit not only joins me in this prayer but also prays on behalf of my kids. He champions them! Oh how we need His strength in our weakness, His guidance in our prayer lives, and His groaning on our behalf, all for the good of our kids and the glory of God.

DAY 4

HE IS BETTER THAN SELF-HELP

There are a few things I've learned along the way, and one of them is this: Don't go running with a runner if you're not one. Just flat out say no thank you and be on your way. And if she persists, because you're staying with her for the weekend, well then, swallow your pride but take her offer to borrow her bike and pedal alongside her.

This might be the true story of what happened when I was staying with my friend Elisabeth for the weekend.

Before we left the house for what I will call our "bike and run," I overheard her tell her husband we'd be back in about an hour or two—and that's when I knew I was really in trouble. Who runs for an hour ... *or two*? But there's little I won't do to get time with this friend who no longer lives down the street but across many states. So off we went.

About twenty minutes into our bike and run, on a beautiful trail near her home, I noticed a huge hill straight ahead (that would be better called a mountain because it was so steep), and all I could think was, *Surely there's a path to the left or to the right where she plans to take me.* But no. She ran straight for it. "Woman," I said with great exasperation, "what exactly is the plan here?" She smiled and pointed, "We're going up it. Come on. I've got your back!" Uh-huh. I apologized to my quads and started to pedal with all my might. I also tried to recall the breathing techniques I learned in childbirthing classes, which this experience was starting to resemble.

I want to tell you I made it up the hill without help. I can feel you cheering for me, and I don't want to let you down. But I didn't make it, at least not on my own. My thighs were burning, and my face was an unbecoming shade of purple, but there was no way was I going to ask for help. But without saying a word, Elisabeth placed her hand on the small of my back and kindly said "Come on, sister, we've got this! We're not quitting. We can do this." Goodbye, pride.

Isn't so much of life—and parenting—like that hill? When we see the mountains before us, we just take a deep breath and pedal with all our might. We don't want to admit weakness or need. We just determine to press in and pull it off.

But the truth is, we need help. A lot of help. We need the championing of our Helper, the Holy Spirit!

Where do you need the Spirit's help in a hill that's before you? Your answer may have everything or nothing to do with your children at this moment.

John 14:16 tells us that the Holy Spirit is our "Helper." The original Greek word for this is *parakletos*, meaning one who has been summoned to come to our aid—"of the Holy Spirit destined ... to lead them [that's us!] to a deeper knowledge of the gospel truth, and give them divine strength needed to enable them to undergo trials and persecutions on behalf of the divine kingdom."[30]

I left you quite a bit of space to answer that question, and maybe that's because I feel like I could fill entire pages with my own answer. But now I want to follow up with another question that's going to require more honest reflection.

Are you accepting the help? And if not, what keeps you from taking His help or even asking for it?

The truth is, most of us attempt to get through life without asking for the Holy Spirit's guidance, and oftentimes we don't even realize it. Or—and this might hit a nerve—we have bought into the story that self-help is the answer.

In our desire to have more strength in our struggles and more control over our circumstances, we might listen to voices who swear the answer is found in striving to be the superheroes of our stories. We are encouraged to give ourselves pep talks about our own greatness, all for our own glory. All the while, the Spirit of Almighty God indwells us and is eager to empower us to fight our battles in His might for His name.

God has given us the Holy Spirit's indwelling to help us along, so let's stop settling for doing it alone.

SELF-HELP VS. SPIRIT-HELP

In *Merriam-Webster*, *self-help* is defined as "the action or process of bettering oneself or overcoming one's problems without the aid of others."[31] But God didn't design us to grow in His likeness or navigate life's problems without the help of His Spirit. We were designed by our Creator to live empowered by His Spirit.

Jesus relied on the empowerment of His Spirit. The disciples relied on the empowerment of the Holy Spirit. So why wouldn't we? We are settling for so much less than what the Spirit can do in our lives (and in our children's lives) when we rely only on what we bring to the table.

We forego witnessing the supernatural when we choose self-help over Spirit-help.

And here's the other thing. When Elisabeth put her hand on the small of my back while I was pedaling uphill, she gave me the gentle push I needed. But what she did for me drastically pales in comparison to what the Spirit does. This is no gentle push on the small of our backs. This is the power of God—that raised Jesus from the dead—strengthening us in our inner beings.

THE PURPOSE OF SPIRIT-HELP
OPEN YOUR BIBLE and read Ephesians 3:14-21.

What did Paul pray for in verse 16, and how did Paul say this would happen?

Why did Paul want us to experience this Spirit-given strengthening in our inner being?

Paul prayed that we may be strengthened with power through the Spirit *so that* we might know the love that changes everything. So that we might know all that we have in Jesus. So that we might know how wide and deep and high and long is God's love for us. His love is transformative, empowering, and fills us with His fullness. And all of this happens through the power of the Holy Spirit!

This is the truest thing I know: Jesus is life; His love is better, and He is the answer to every longing we fill with lesser things that only leave us feeling empty again.

We *get to* be filled with the fullness of God, which is the only thing that satisfies the human soul. We don't need more self-love; we need more Savior-love.

THE SAVIOR'S LOVE

Only the Savior's love has the power to propel us into radical life change, and here is why: The Savior's love, proven in His sacrifice on the cross, invites us to anchor our identity in something that has already been established, not in something we are striving to attain. What is established is your identity as a child of God, created on purpose for a purpose. You are known by God, valuable to God, treasured by God, and welcomed by God. Out of this identity you are empowered by the Spirit to live courageously into the calling God puts on your life.

Our identity in Christ empowers us not only to say with our lips but believe in our hearts: "I am who He says I am, and I am equipped to do what He's called me to do by His Spirit who lives in me."

I want to invite you to write that last sentence down, speak it out loud, and ask the Holy Spirit to impress it on your heart!

The only love that can bring wholeness is the love that Jesus proved through giving His life on the cross. No amount of self-love will ever be enough to satisfy the ache in your heart or the brokenness in your life. Our Savior, in His love for us, gave us the Spirit to guide our hearts so that we can know His love for us every moment of every day.

I want us to pause here and think about how this pertains to parenting and our messaging with our kids. If your children are of the age to have electronic devices and have access to platforms where everyone is striving to prove they are worthy of love and belonging, you know how hard this is on their hearts. You see your kids trying to be more lovable so they are invited to the table. You probably see them searching for love and affirmation anywhere it can be found.

> How are you seeing the pressure to prove your worth impacting your kids?

Unwavering Savior-love is a pivotal truth for us to own and pass down if we want our kids to live freely in the full understanding of His love and purpose for their lives. Our kids need to grasp that all believers have been transformed to live in agreement with our new status as God's children. They have nothing left to prove! Not to themselves and not to anyone else. Even on their most unlovable days, they are loved unconditionally by God because of Jesus. And the Spirit enables them to live like this is true!

OPEN YOUR BIBLE and read 1 Corinthians 6:19-20.

What does this passage tell us we should do with our bodies?

We don't have the authority to determine our worth. But, friend, this is good news because our sense of worth and value ebbs and flows with what we do and don't accomplish or how well we do or don't walk faithfully with Christ. This sense of worth is based on our flesh that fails. The One who holds *all* authority has called us worthy—worthy of the sacrifice of His Son and the indwelling of His Spirit. We were bought with a price. We are not our own.

You are washed, clean, forgiven, and free. Free from guilt and shame over your sin and inadequacy. You are redeemed and righteous before our holy God.

The worth we long to feel is found in resting in Jesus' love, not in more self-love. We don't need to do a better job loving ourselves. Let me explain.

By no means should we see ourselves as "worthless." It's quite the opposite. The Lord wants us to have a healthy self-image anchored in the truth that we are made in His image. God is clear—you are of great worth in his eyes:

> *And the very hairs on your head are all numbered. So don't be afraid;*
> *you are more valuable to God than a whole flock of sparrows.*
> LUKE 12:7, NLT

But nowhere in Scripture do we find God telling us to do a better job of "loving ourselves." Rather, we read in 1 John 4:16 (NIV):

> *And so we know and rely on the love God has for us.*

Read that verse again. What are we to "know and rely on"?

"Self-love is one of our highest forms of self-deception: we gorge ourselves on the biblical truth of our human worth—being created in God's image (Gen. 1:26)—but refuse to swallow the balancing truth that our own sin has robbed us of loveliness. Self-love is fundamentally unsatisfactory and lacking, because we are somehow expected to ignore half of who we are as sinful humans."[32]

Here are just a few verses to assure us of the condition of our sinful nature:

- We are dead in our sin (Eph. 2:1; Rom. 5:12).
- Not one human is perfect (Ps. 14:3).
- Everyone is guilty of breaking God's commands (Jas. 2:10).
- Scripture has shut up all people under sin (Gal. 3:22).
- Every intent of the thoughts of humankind's hearts were only evil continually (Gen. 6:5).
- The human heart cannot solely be trusted (Jer. 17:9)
- Humans are born with sinful natures (Ps. 51:5).
- We all fall short of God's glory (Rom. 3:23).

And yet! Here is the good news of our identity in Christ:

- You are fearfully and wonderfully made (Ps. 139:14).
- You are created in the very image of your Father (Gen. 1:27).
- You were chosen before the foundation of the world to be God's beloved, adopted, accepted, redeemed, and forgiven children (Eph. 1:3-8).
- You are the King's kid (1 John 3:1).
- You're a friend of God (John 15:12-15).
- You're the apple of His eye (Ps. 17:8).
- You are delighted in and celebrated over (Zeph. 3:17).
- You are an heir of God and coheir with Christ (Rom. 8:16-17).
- You are His masterpiece, created in Christ to do the good things He planned for you long ago (Eph. 2:8-11).

The Spirit empowers us to live out of our new identity in Christ. He helps us live propelled by Christ's love!

Share what this is stirring in you. Why can this be so difficult to digest? Or perhaps it's not difficult for you. Perhaps you are shouting a hallelujah and amen! Explain.

How have you experienced this kind of identity shift in your own life? Moving from living like you have to prove your worth and lovability, to living like your worth and lovability have already been proven in Jesus, freeing you to live in confidence as a child of God?

This is what happened to me almost ten years ago, and it's no exaggeration to say I've never been the same. I think it's why I am so passionate about this point. We invest so much of our mental capacity trying to fix ourselves and help ourselves and love ourselves, while the Spirit is saying, *I'm here to help. I can do far more than you imagine. Let Me assure you of your value. Let Me do what God has given Me to do in you and for you!*

Read 1 Corinthians 6:19-20 again. What do these verses teach you about what God can do through His Spirit within you?

Often, instead of expecting the Spirit to manifest His supernatural power and do far more abundantly than we can imagine, we mostly just pedal faster and puff harder to get up the hill.

One of the biggest mistakes we can make is underestimating the Spirit.

What step or steps could you make today to become more reliant on the Spirit rather than on yourself?

Let me be clear: My intention isn't to undermine the myriad ways we can be bettered by taking intentional steps to grow. To make progress, we must be willing to put in the effort. This is biblical.

LIVE AS LIGHT
Philippians 2:12-13 (NLT) says,

> *Dear friends, you always followed my instructions when I was with you. And now that I am away, it is even more important. Work hard to show the results of your salvation, obeying God with deep reverence and fear. For God is working in you, giving you the desire and the power to do what pleases him.*

Notice what Paul said we should do and what he said we can count on God to do.

What is our role in our spiritual growth?

Yes, we're tasked with working hard. We're commissioned to revere and fear God. But as we do, we must know that we aren't working alone! God and God alone gives us two things:

Fill in the blanks based on Philippians 2:13 (NLT).

"For God is working _____ you, _____ you the _____ and the _____ to do what pleases Him."

Desire without power is useless. And power without desire is pointless. But by the power of His Spirit in you, God freely gives you both. He doesn't make you work for it or earn it. He freely gives it.

It's only in pleasing God through the Spirit's guidance and power that we, as His children, will become more and more of who He made us to be, both as women and as mothers.

Here's the other thing. We have to stop trying to be the savior of our own stories if we want our lives to give God the glory.

The Spirit helps us like no superhero cape tied around our neck ever could. I mean, yes, it's fun and helpful to flex our muscles, repeat a few affirming mantras, and drink out of a mug that tells us we're boss babes, but that only gets us so far. Yes, it gets us somewhere we weren't before, but only the really honest will admit it's not as far as we'd like to go. It's not freedom from relying on the flesh to do what only the Spirit can accomplish.

When Jesus was teaching in the synagogue in Capernaum on being the Bread of life, He said,

> *What gives life is God's Spirit; human power is of no use at all.*
> JOHN 6:63, GNT

Human power is no use in producing salvation or sanctification. We can't save ourselves, and we can't change ourselves—at least not to the extent that we need or want.

True transformation comes only through God alone.

Do you want to know what I believe is the best self-help strategy? Admitting how much the self needs God! We need Him for authentic, lasting, radical change. Self-reliance, self-confidence, self-love, self-sufficiency, self-anything falls short of what the Spirit can accomplish through us if we will allow Him to work in us.

HOW DOES THIS EMPOWER MY PARENTING?

How are the biblical truths we uncovered today going to impact how you parent your children around this conversation about self-love and identifying as God's children?

What makes it difficult, if anything, to speak openly with our children about the reality of our sinful nature?

How does the bad news of our sinful nature lead our kids to the good news of our sinless Savior?

We are free to confess when we fail because God's love is unfailing!

The more our children see this freedom in us, the more likely they will be to walk in this freedom themselves. Our freedom will be contagious, and through it, they will come to know the power of God's love through the Holy Spirit to navigate the valleys of life and climb the hills on the path.

#NeverAloneBibleStudy

THE SANCTIFYING OF THE HOLY SPIRIT

In our family we have an expression known as the "Holy Spirit nudge." Sometimes His nudge guides us to do something or to say something, and sometimes that nudge tells us not to do or say something else. It's the check in our spirit that urges "do this" or "stop that," "say this" or "stay quiet," or "keep going" or "wait."

For example, I have experienced the Spirit's conviction when I'm about to share a story about someone and a thought interrupts me that says, *You don't need to share this story. It's just gossip and nobody wins.* Or when my kids are arguing and I'm at my wits' end and ready to let unkind words roll off my tongue, then a Bible verse interrupts me before I unleash: "If someone is caught in a sin, you who live by the Spirit should restore that person gently" (Gal. 6:1, NIV). Or when I'm harboring bitterness and the Holy Spirit reminds me of the undeserved forgiveness I have in Jesus. Or when I see an opportunity to be the love of Jesus to a stranger and I sense "do this!"

In the spirit of complete transparency, I will confess that sometimes I heed the nudge and sometimes I don't. And then I either reap the benefits or clean up the mess. I bet you can relate.

The truth is, we need the conviction of the Spirit to keep us on the right path, to guide us in obedience, to make us more like Jesus, and ultimately to produce fruit in our lives that brings others to Him. These are the sanctifying works of the Spirit that we will be studying this week. Let's get started!

DAY 1
HE CONVICTS US

Of the multitude of things we must teach our kids while they're under our care, there's one powerful benefit of the Holy Spirit that we need to share intentionally with our kids. It's our job to help our children identify the Spirit's convicting work in their lives. As believers, we all want our children to walk in righteousness and turn from the sin that tempts them, but this is only possible as our children learn how to heed the Spirit's voice of conviction. This lesson is invaluable as we prepare them to launch into adulthood.

For example, when I discover that my son was dishonest with me, I might ask him if there was a nudge in his spirit that was making him uncomfortable when he was lying. Then I explain to him that was the Holy Spirit. Or when I discover another son made a choice that wasn't in alignment with who God calls him to be, I will ask him if he felt a pang of guilt in the midst of his action. Then I remind him that was the Holy Spirit calling him to repentance and forgiveness. Or when I see my other son choose self-control when I know his temper wants to win, I affirm how he yielded to the Holy Spirit and displayed the character of Christ.

The conviction of the Holy Spirit is one of the gifts we should be most grateful for in our kids' lives, but instead, it may be the one that many of us most take for granted—by "for granted" I mean that we try to play this role in our kids' lives rather than relying on the Holy Spirit to do His good work in them. I know I do! But I don't tend to convict like the Holy Spirit. I try to prick their consciences with persuasive words or change their choices with consequences. But that's not how the Holy Spirit convicts.

Of course we must train our children in righteousness and help them understand what's going on in their hearts when they sin. But today I hope we will learn more about the difference in our role and the Spirit's role in helping our children not only recognize, but run from sin.

> Do you ever find yourself trying to play the Spirit's role of conviction in your child's life? What does that look like? What does it produce?

The word *convict* is a translation of the Greek word *elenchō*, which means "to bring a person to the point of recognizing wrongdoing. To convince someone of something."[33] And this is what the Holy Spirit delights to do in us and in our children. He convicts us by exposing our sin in the light of God's love and convincing us of our need for the saving work of Jesus.

Why is it so easy to forget that we aren't alone in our effort to help our children see the truthfulness of God's Word and the preciousness of Christ? We know in our minds that it's the Holy Spirit's work alone to convict our kids, but we sometimes parent like the work is ours. At least that's true for me. I too easily believe the lie that it's all on me to convince my child to choose obedience to Christ and to conform my child into the image of Christ, which only results in fear and frustration. But the truth is, the burden of conviction doesn't belong to me. And it doesn't belong to you either.

HOW DOES THE SPIRIT CONVICT US?

We are returning to the passage we read on our very first day of study, the one where Jesus said to His disciples, "It is to your advantage that I go away so the Helper will come" (my paraphrase). But what we haven't studied is the very next thing Jesus said about what the Helper would do when He came. This is the good stuff we will study today.

OPEN YOUR BIBLE and read John 16:5-11.

Jesus taught that the Holy Spirit would convict believers of "sin and righteousness and judgment" (v. 8). We are going to take these three things one by one and apply them to our parenting. Ready?

CONCERNING SIN

The Spirit convicting us concerning sin means the Spirit convinces us we need Jesus because of our sin. Once we put our trust in Jesus, His conviction continues. The Holy Spirit's job is to go on illuminating our sinfulness, convincing us of its harmfulness, and persuading us to choose obedience. His conviction is intended to protect us from the pain and harm that sin inflicts on our lives and on the lives of people around us, and to show us the ways in which sin separates us from God's best for us. His purpose is to turn us away from sin and to make us more like Jesus.

What is the Holy Spirit's job, according to the paragraph you just read?

The Holy Spirit convicts unsaved people. Without His converting work, there would be no Christians!

The work of the Spirit to convict doesn't mean parents are off the hook. There is hard and holy work to be done. Discipleship is the most important job we have as parents—grounding our family in God's Word, getting on our knees in prayer, and being the hands and feet of Jesus as a family. We have to partner with the Spirit in planting gospel seeds. But the onus isn't on us. We need to know that. Our most persuasive speech cannot convince our kids of their need for Jesus. This is actually not an easy pill to swallow for me, because I want to be able to convince my kids that the gospel is life and Jesus is better. But then I remember that their Father God longs for them to know His heart for them even more than I do, and I am freed to once again trust Him with His children.

It's the Holy Spirit's job to convince your kids of their need for Jesus. And it's the Spirit who continues illuminating sinful and destructive behaviors to your kids.

> How have you explained this role of the Spirit to your kids? Or how can you begin to explain this role to your kids if you haven't already?

> What can you do as a mom to partner with the Holy Spirit in the convicting work He wants to do in your kids?

Another thing we need to know is that conviction is not condemnation. How do we know the difference? Conviction comes from the Advocate; condemnation comes from the accuser.

Conviction leads to reconciliation with God and man. It is the Spirit's work of love in our lives.

His conviction is intended to conform us into the image of Jesus Christ.

Condemnation comes from the enemy. The messaging is shaming and accusatory, and it results in us running from Jesus in fear rather than to Him for forgiveness and reconciliation.

Put in your own words the difference between using convicting language and condemning language in your parenting to reflect the heart of God.

This doesn't mean the Spirit's conviction will always feel good. He has to show us how unlovely our sin is before our Almighty God. Oftentimes, when the Spirit convicts me, it's painful and produces good guilt because I have to face how I've grieved God with my disobedience. But His conviction never leaves us feeling guilty. It leads us to the good news of our acquittal.

CONCERNING RIGHTEOUSNESS

Reread John 16:10. Why did Jesus say the Holy Spirit would convict us concerning righteousness? What was the "because" Jesus gave in verse 10?

Watch how this goes down.

The Holy Spirit convicts us of our sin, showing us how impossible it is to meet God's high moral standard, which isn't only perfection in our outward actions but perfection in our hearts. God's law requires more than good external behavior. His high standard is a pure and perfect heart. A heart that loves Him above all else.

This is the heart of Jesus' message in Matthew 23:27-28:

> *Woe to you, scribes and Pharisees, hypocrites!*
> *For you are like whitewashed tombs, which outwardly appear*
> *beautiful, but within are full of dead people's bones and all*
> *uncleanness. So you also outwardly appear righteous to*
> *others, but within you are full of hypocrisy and lawlessness.*

How did Jesus describe the Pharisees' outsides? And their insides?

Pharisees were very proud of their self-proclaimed perfect keeping of the Law, but Jesus called them out on their works-based righteousness.

He taught that doing the right thing with the wrong motive still fails to meet the moral standard called for in Jesus' Sermon on the Mount. So even if we think we are getting it all right in our outward actions, we aren't getting it all right in our hearts—at least not to the extent that God demands. This is what the Spirit does for us—He shows us that works-based righteousness doesn't justify us. But what seems like bad news is actually the doorway to the good news!

The Holy Spirit counsels us that the complete righteousness God requires was satisfied by Jesus. Jesus was not only pure and perfect in His outward behavior, He also was pure and perfect in His heart on our behalf. And only because of Him are we declared righteous before God! This means we are made right with God because we are covered in the perfection of His Son.

OPEN YOUR BIBLE and read what Paul wrote in 2 Corinthians 5:21.

How do we become the righteousness of God?

The Holy Spirit reveals our brokenness so that we will finally be set free from trying to achieve an unachievable righteousness. He reveals our desperation so that we will fall in awe and wonder at the feet of the One who achieved righteousness for us.

The Holy Spirit shows us our security in our Savior. That sense of peace we experience about our salvation is the work of the Holy Spirit.

Have you ever feared that God might turn His back on you, or worse, abandon you because you keep stumbling into that same sin? Explain.

God wants to free you from that fear, and He is the only One who can. Without the Spirit's reassurance of our imputed righteousness, it would be impossible to believe. The grace is too great for us to comprehend!

Mamas, we aren't the only ones in pursuit of works-based righteousness. We aren't the only ones trying to put on a perfect performance for other people's approval or for God's acceptance. Our kids are doing it too. They, too, fall for the enemy's lie that God only loves them when they're getting it right. Or maybe our kids are trying to keep God's wrath at bay by their pursuit of good behavior. Or worse, they've given up because they believe they'll never be as good as God expects.

> How do you model for your children that our desperate condition is a beautiful invitation to fall on the mercy and love of Jesus?

CONCERNING JUDGMENT
Reread John 16:11.

To say the Holy Spirit convicts us concerning judgment means that Satan, the former ruler of this world, has already been judged and stands condemned through Jesus' death. Satan is living on borrowed time—his demise is inevitable.

> Read the verses below and record what you learn from each one.

> John 12:31:

> John 14:30:

But it is also the Spirit's role to convict us of final judgment when "we must all appear before the judgment seat of Christ" (2 Cor. 5:10). This conviction is meant to produce holy fear in us to honor God with our lives. Even this work of the Spirit is for our benefit; it reminds us that we are being held accountable for our actions and that this world will one day come to an end. Satan's not invincible, and neither are we. So we must make the most of the time we have. But while we're being mindful of our time and choices, there's an important distinction to make: When Satan tempts you to believe that your sinful nature still holds authority over you, remind him whose power resides inside you. The Spirit of Almighty God! Through the indwelling Holy Spirit, you have the supernatural power to defeat the enemy's temptation. Victory is yours in Jesus' name.

We are fighting a battle that has already been won!

But do our kids know this? Do we talk about this in our homes? For example, one of my boys recently expressed frustration over a continual temptation in his life—one he feels like he will never win. His confession led to a powerful conversation about how the power of the Spirit at work inside him is greater than the pull of sin at work against him! (See 1 John 4:4.)

> What messaging can you weave into your conversations with your kids to help your children remember that the one inside them is greater than the one working against them?

HOW DO I KNOW IT'S THE HOLY SPIRIT?

A question our growing kids will likely ask (if they haven't yet) is, "How can I tell the difference in the Holy Spirit's conviction and my human conscience?" Or maybe that's even a question you're asking now.

> Look up the Scripture passages below and record what each teaches about the human conscience.
>
> Titus 1:15:
>
> Hebrews 10:22:
>
> 1 Timothy 4:1-2:

Our consciences only carry us so far. Our consciences are "evil" (Heb. 10:22). They can't be trusted because they are corrupt with sin and informed by our circumstances. Our consciences may give us a pass on something the Spirit would not. In fact, they could even lead us to "depart from the faith" (1 Tim. 4:1).

The difference in the human conscience and the Holy Spirit is that the Holy Spirit can always be trusted because He speaks only what He hears from God. This is a benefit we previously studied in John 16:13 (NIV):

> *But when he, the Spirit of truth, comes, he will guide you into all the truth. He will not speak on his own; he will speak only what he hears, and he will tell you what is yet to come.*

Can the Holy Spirit use our consciences to convict us? Absolutely. Can He conform our consciences to God's? He can and does! "We have the mind of Christ" (1 Cor. 2:16). The Holy Spirit fills our human spirit and works from the inside out. His presence emanates into our souls, influencing our mind, will, and emotions. But wait, there's more! The Spirit doesn't just fill our old humanity (that would be new wine in old wineskins); He recreates our humanity in Christ. We are new creations, born again into Christ's resurrected humanity.

A person without the indwelling Holy Spirit can only function from the human conscience.

But a person indwelt with the Spirit has the mind of Christ and will hear the Spirit's voice and know the Spirit's nudge.

> Identify times when you have felt His nudge. In each circumstance, how did you know it was the Holy Spirit?

HOW DOES THIS EMPOWER MY PARENTING?

> How would you describe the difference in our role and the Holy Spirit's role in what we've studied today?

> How does recognizing this difference impact the pressure you might feel to help your children recognize their need for Jesus and the harmfulness of sin?

Make it your aim today to be aware of opportunities to point out the Spirit's presence and good work of conviction in your kids' lives. If our children have put their faith in Jesus, let's never miss an opportunity to say, "That was the Spirit of God in you!" And if we are still praying for our children to put their trust in Jesus, let us put our confidence in the Spirit's convicting work to show them their need for Jesus!

HE EMPOWERS US TO OBEY

When our boys were little and they would resist the rules we established for them, I began the practice of saying to them, "I require obedience *from* you because I am *for* you." The message was, "I am on your team, I am in your corner; I don't give you rules to hold you back; I give you rules to propel you into who God made you to be. The boundaries are for your benefit."

Cue the eye roll from my kids, but as grown-ups on the other side of adolescence we know this to be true. So why do we doubt that God's call to obedience from us is any different? He asks for obedience from us because He is for us. God's "rules" are rooted in love, and they are always for our good.

I know that for many, either because of their upbringing or from hearing false teaching, the word *obedience* paints a picture of a strict God who just likes keeping us in line rather than a loving God who gives us abundant life. I hope today's conversation will help us see—and teach our kids—how everything He asks of us is because He is for us.

> What was your experience growing up? Did obedience to God feel like it was something for your benefit or for your boredom?

> Or perhaps you weren't raised in a home where living in obedience to God was part of the conversation. If that's the case, where did you form your opinion of why God gives us instructions for life?

God's desire is for us to obey out of love and gratitude rather than guilt and obligation. For our obedience to be motivated by love and gratitude, we need to meditate on the unmerited love He first showed us in Jesus: "We love because He first loved us" (1 John 4:19). A heart softened by the gospel becomes a heart surrendered and submitted to God.

THE SPIRIT GIVES US THE DESIRE TO OBEY

How does this happen? How are our hearts softened by the gospel? The Holy Spirit! The Holy Spirit softens our hearts by making Jesus beautiful to us.

John Piper puts it this way:

> *"If we want freedom from our blindness to the Beauty of God, we must have the Spirit. We are slaves to the worldly substitutes for divine Beauty until the Spirit takes the veil from our minds and grants us to see with joy the Beauty of the Lord. ... When a person turns to Jesus Christ as Lord and opens himself up to the liberating rule of the Spirit of the Lord, two of his deepest longings begin to be fulfilled. It is granted that the eyes of his heart (Ephesians 1:18) really see a captivating and satisfying divine Beauty. And he begins to be changed by it. We always tend to become like the persons we admire. And when the Spirit grants us to see and admire the Lord of Glory, we inevitably begin to be transformed into his image. And the more we become like him, the more clearly we can see him, and the greater our capacity to delight in his beauty."*[34]

The more beautiful Jesus becomes, the more I desire to live a life that honors Him and reflects His love. Obedience will feel burdensome until Jesus is beautiful.

How have you experienced this to be true in your own life?

As a parent I'm often tempted to resort to threats of painful consequences to motivate good behavior. Giving consequences for our child's disobedience is right and good and biblical. I'm not suggesting otherwise. But I am challenging us to think about the difference in how we tend to rely on consequences for behavior change in light of how the Holy Spirit relies on a heart melted by the gospel. We all have moments (and plenty of them!) when the stress of parenting becomes too much, but it's in those times when we must remain focused on how the Father has chosen to parent us. Despite His holy anger at our stubborn or ignorant ways, He motivates us with forgiveness, love, and grace.

Grace is the unearned and undeserved favor of God. It is the means by which God saves, sustains, sanctifies, and strengthens us in the Person and work of Jesus Christ. Grace is God looking at our sin—the gravity and magnitude of it—and out of His great love, choosing to give us Jesus to atone for it.

This is how we know what love is: Jesus Christ laid down His life for us.
1 JOHN 3:16, NIV

The question for us as moms is, how can we partner with the Holy Spirit in revealing Jesus' grace to our kids?

> Reflect and record times when have you seen grace produce internal heart change in your child.

Also remember, the fruit of grace-based parenting is rarely immediate. It can take weeks, months, years before we see the fruit from the seeds we plant. As my husband has to remind me often, this is not a sprint. Would we rather force fake fruit in the present or wait patiently on the Spirit to transform their hearts with God's grace?

This doesn't mean we don't discipline our kids. God "disciplines those he loves" (Prov. 3:12; Heb. 12:6, NIV). No, grace isn't a lack of discipline and consequences. It's the unconditional love of God woven into it. It's about parenting our children the way God parents us and emulating His grace in everything we do. Grace motivates!

But we know we need more than motivation to obey. We also need power. So the Holy Spirit gives us this too.

THE SPIRIT ENABLES US TO OBEY
OPEN YOUR BIBLE and read 2 Peter 1:3-11 (NIV).

This passage is so rich, so we are going to camp out here and unpack it.

> Fill in the blanks as we work through each verse.
>
> *In verse 3, Peter said that God's divine power—which is the Holy Spirit—has given us _____ we need for a godly life.*

God hasn't given us "some" of what we need. He's given us "everything" we need, because He knows how much we're prone to wander and lose our way.

> *In verse 4, Peter spoke of how we partake of God's divine power. It is through His great and precious _____.*

In other words, by receiving and believing the gospel we are equipped with the Spirit's power for obedience. This means Jesus has promised us that we do not fight this battle against sin alone.

In verses 5-7, Peter urged believers to make _____ _____ to add to our faith qualities that are consistent with who we are in Christ.

Do you see how Peter affirmed that we play a vital role in obedience? The Holy Spirit empowers our obedience, but it still requires our effort. We must be committed to our own spiritual growth if we want the Spirit's work in us to be effective. This transformation isn't completed at a certain age or stage. Our growth should be continual and regularly evaluated.

Now look at verses 8-10 and notice what Peter attributed to why people do not put effort, or simply stop putting effort, into obedience.

Forgetting or disregarding the grace given to us in Jesus Christ through the forgiveness of sins is what causes us to slip into lazy, self-centered, and sinful living.

But the Holy Spirit awakens us to the breathtaking beauty of God's grace to compel us toward obedience. When we experience these increasing qualities, we become encouraged to further our growth, in turn strengthening our confidence in our faith, confirming God's call upon our lives, and resting in the knowledge that we "will never stumble" (2 Pet. 1:10, NIV) outside of heaven's grasp.

How have you experienced this to be true in your life?

Paul said something similar in 1 Corinthians 15:10 (NIV):

But by the grace of God I am what I am, and his grace to me was not without effect. No, I worked harder than all of them—yet not I, but the grace of God that was with me.

Grace isn't a scapegoat for obedience but a stimulator of obedience.

God's grace rescued Paul, and the effect was the desire to obey God by the power of the Holy Spirit. He said "not I" because He knew it was the Holy Spirit inside him that enabled him in his calling. "Not I" also demonstrates that Paul didn't want the glory for who he became and how he obeyed. More proof that the Holy Spirit was at work in Paul.

> Pause and pray, asking the Holy Spirit to give you fresh empowerment in your effort to obey your Father. Now ask the Holy Spirit to do the same in the hearts of your children.

The reality is, we need this prayer on repeat because there is a very real battle going on for the affection of our hearts.

THE SPIRIT GUIDES US
Read Galatians 5:16-17 (NLT) below.

> *Let the Holy Spirit guide your lives. Then you won't be doing what your sinful nature craves. The sinful nature wants to do evil, which is just the opposite of what the Spirit wants. And the Spirit gives us desires that are the opposite of what the sinful nature desires. These two forces are constantly fighting each other, so you are not free to carry out your good intentions.*

> Why do we need to let the Holy Spirit guide us?

> What does the Spirit give us?

We need the Spirit's help because our sinful nature is hostile to the Spirit. The only way to obey is by letting the Spirit guide us and grant us power.

> Do you feel your sinful nature battling with the Spirit? Explain.

Do you know who desperately needs to know this? Our kids! We must talk to them about the battle being waged.

I've said shaming things to my kids when they would sin without realizing what I was doing. I've used words that suggest they aren't subject to the very real battle of the flesh and Spirit. When in truth, our kids, like us, are messy, complicated sinners who have a sinful nature that wants to keep them from carrying out their good intentions. And this will be their story, and our story, until Jesus returns and completes His work in us.

But that's not the end of this story.

OPEN YOUR BIBLE and read Galatians 5:25.

Where the Holy Spirit leads, we must follow. Where He guides, we must go. If we "keep in step with the Spirit," then we have the power to defeat the sinful nature. But keeping in step with the Spirit won't just happen to us. It requires action, effort.

However, if we sidestep the Spirit, we step right into the enemy's snare and succumb to what the sinful nature craves. When we sin, we are not yielded to the empowering of the Holy Spirit. We are neglecting His presence and forgoing His power, allowing the sinful nature to win.

We need to be teaching our kids that we don't fight alone. We have the authority and the victory in the Spirit to say, "Back up, Satan!" We can call the devil out. Make it personal, because it is personal.

But we also need to be teaching our kids there are consequences to sidestepping the Spirit.

OPEN YOUR BIBLE and read Galatians 6:7,9.

What will we harvest?

Why should we not tire of doing what is good?

Paul wasn't advocating a karma mentality, as some assume from this passage. He was acknowledging that when we sow to the flesh, we will bear the consequence of our sin. But when we stay in step with the Spirit, we will reap the righteousness of God.

In closing today, I want to encourage us with something Jesus said to His disciples about the spirit and the flesh. On the night before His death, Jesus went with His disciples to a place called Gethsemane to pray, and He said to them, "My soul is overwhelmed with sorrow to the point of death. Stay here and keep watch with me" (Matt. 26:38, NIV). But instead of keeping watch with Him, they fell asleep. When He found them sleeping, He woke them and said, "The spirit is willing, but the flesh is weak" (v. 41, NIV).

In this passage, Jesus spoke of the human spirit, not the Holy Spirit. The word for "spirit" here is the Greek word *pneuma*, which, in this context, refers to the soul and mind of man. *Pneuma* is "the disposition or influence which fills and governs the soul of any one," or, in other words, our "source of any power, affection, emotion, desire."[35] Our *pneuma* wants to do good. The word "flesh" here refers to our human nature in all of its frailty. So while our human spirit may try to muster up what it takes, our human flesh fails.

See, Jesus didn't shame or condemn them. Instead, Jesus acknowledged what was true of them in the garden of Gethsemane and what is true of us and our kids today. Our spirit is willing but our flesh is weak. Our effort, though required, isn't enough. Jesus renews our humanity by taking our weakness upon Himself and living rightly in our place. In the power of the Spirit, we are new creations in Christ to walk in obedience to our God.

HOW DOES THIS EMPOWER MY PARENTING?
Once our children put their faith in Jesus, it's empowering for them to understand that they have a choice. They can sidestep the Spirit, ignoring His nudge and discounting His voice, but that choice is not without consequence. Or they can keep in step with the Spirit by heeding His nudge and following His voice, and experience the blessing that comes with obedience.

What stuns me—but it shouldn't because God is so good—is that even when we satisfy the flesh, the Spirit won't cease to exercise His loving conviction in our lives. Our choices may grieve Him and impede Him, but they can't make Him quit. The Holy Spirit is no quitter. He will always have our back when we need to fight sin.

> Is there a battle your child is presently in? What sin fights for their affection and attention? Let us not neglect the privilege of pointing them to the Guide who wants to keep them on the path of abundant life.

DAY 3
HE MAKES US MORE LIKE JESUS

My son Brennan thinks deeply about things, and he asks such good questions. He doesn't accept rote answers tied up in pretty bows, and though that can cause doubt in his youth, I am expectant that this will only strengthen his faith as he matures and continues to encounter the faithfulness of Jesus.

Recently, while I was driving him to youth group and we were chatting about what they'd been learning, he asked one of his good questions: "Mom, how do I know if I'm growing in my faith?" (Hello, Holy Spirit, I need your help!)

It was such a good question that I thought even the Holy Spirit would need a minute to give me a good answer (I kid!), so I delayed my answer by telling Brennan in all manner of ways how much I love how deeply he thinks about things.

> I wonder, even now, how you would answer that question.
> Write down what comes to mind.

Before I answered, I asked Brennan if he had any ideas about what growth looks like. Our conversation became a beautiful back and forth about what it looks like to grow in our relationship with Jesus and for our lives to grow in the likeness of Jesus.

It also opened the door for me to talk with Brennan about how the Holy Spirit helps him grow in his faith and in holiness. This is what the Bible calls sanctification. Growth, or sanctification, can't be simplified to "becoming a better Christian." It's really about becoming more and more aware of how much we need the work of Jesus and the power of the Spirit to help us obey the Father. And then seeking to please Him more than indulge our sin. That is growth.

HE REFINES US
The English word *sanctification* comes from the Greek word *hagiasmós*, which means to "set apart" for a purpose.[36] To sanctify is to make holy. So sanctification is the ongoing process of the Holy Spirit growing us in holiness.

Read 2 Thessalonians 2:13 below:

> But we ought always to give thanks to God for you, brothers beloved by the Lord, because God chose you as the firstfruits to be saved, through sanctification by the Spirit and belief in the truth.

In the verse above, underline who and what is responsible for our sanctification.

Read 1 Corinthians 6:11 below:

> But you were washed, you were sanctified, you were justified in the name of the Lord Jesus Christ and by the Spirit of our God.

Again, in the verse above, underline who's responsible for our sanctification.

I sense that one of the reasons we see so many children launch into the world and leave their faith at home is due to our neglect of the Holy Spirit's role in our sanctification. The Christian life is often viewed as something we must do rather than what's been done for us. We think that in order to be "good Christians" we must work hard at changing our desires and having better behavior. It's all on us and it's all about us. We strive to live like Christ without the power of Christ! We think we have to try hard to make God proud of us, but the harder we try the harder it becomes, and eventually we just give up.

If only we knew the truth! Sanctification is sparked and sustained by remembering what God has done for us in sending Jesus to rescue us and giving us His Spirit to renovate us.

We participate by our obedience, but we don't produce holiness in our lives—He does! Let's talk more about that.

OPEN YOUR BIBLE and read 2 Corinthians 3:17-18.

Fill in the blanks based on what you read.

Where the Spirit is, there is _____.

By _____ the glory of the Lord, we are being

_____ .

This comes from the Lord who is the

_____ .

We are transformed into Jesus' image by beholding Him! And this is the work of the Spirit.

This, Mama, is where we find *freedom*. Freedom from trying to do what He alone is already doing. See the language? We "are being" transformed. It's not "will be." It's already happening. But it's a slow work in us and in our kids. It's from one degree to another. And it won't be completed tomorrow or even while our kids are still under our roofs.

OPEN YOUR BIBLE and read Philippians 1:6.

The Spirit's work in us is good, and it's gonna take time. A lifetime, actually!

> How does this truth change, or perhaps reinforce, how you respond to your child's slow growth?

I hope we're seeing how nowhere in the Bible are we told to make our primary aim being good for God. We are told to behold Him. Trying to be a good Christian was never God's goal for us. His goal is for us to behold His glory. We are changed by knowing Him better, not in trying to be better. The pursuit of Jesus will produce holiness. The closer we get to Jesus, the more we grow in His likeness. We don't change ourselves in that pursuit. The Holy Spirit does.

> Do you spend more time striving to be good for Jesus or seeking to behold Him?

"Whoever says he abides in him ought to walk in the same way in which [Jesus] walked."

1 JOHN 2:6

How has your understanding of sanctification impacted your relationship with Jesus?

How has it impacted the way you parent your children?

Of course, just because the Spirit is the one who sanctifies us doesn't mean we're free to live in intentional sin and expect to still be shaped into the likeness of Jesus.

So let's also look at what Scriptures says about our role in sanctification.

TRUSTING THE PROCESS
Read 1 Thessalonians 5:22-24 below:

> *Abstain from every form of evil. Now may the God of peace himself sanctify you completely, and may your whole spirit and soul and body be kept blameless at the coming of our Lord Jesus Christ. He who calls you is faithful; he will surely do it.*

Write the last sentence of this passage below.

This passage, specifically the sentence you just wrote, is often used to encourage us to be steadfast in what God has called us to do and to trust that He will provide everything we need to fulfill our callings. And this is indeed good encouragement. The God who called you to motherhood will be faithful to carry you through motherhood. (Thank You, Lord!)

But this is not actually what Paul was teaching in this specific passage, as true as it may be.

What did Paul say we should abstain from?

We have a role to play. We have a choice to make. Dabble in sin or abstain from sin. Take the Spirit's help to fight sin or fall into Satan's temptation. The choice is ours, and there's no middle ground. But then Paul clarified who does the sanctifying as we do the obeying.

Reread the whole passage on the previous page and identify who's responsible for sanctifying you.

God Himself, by His Spirit, sanctifies you. This is what Paul was teaching when he wrote, "He who calls you is faithful; He will surely do it" (v. 24).

God who called you to Himself will be faithful to make you more and more like Him—through His Spirit in you—until you are completely perfected at the coming of Jesus.

Where have you witnessed evidence of His sanctification in your life—in desires, in motives, in words, in actions?

How are you resisting the Holy Spirit's sanctifying work?

What are you afraid of losing by surrendering to His work?

Now take a moment to contrast what you're afraid of losing with what you are forfeiting gaining.

How we are called to live as followers of Jesus is how we most fully enjoy the abundant life Jesus came and died to give us.

The way God calls us to live is the outworking of who we already are as new creations in Christ. It's the outworking of our true identity.

OPEN YOUR BIBLE and read Ephesians 4:20-24.

What did Paul say we need to put off?

What do we need to put on?

Putting off the old self "can mean that, once you have become a Christian, you are to leave behind the attitudes, habits, values, and actions that you had before being born again."[37]

To have "learned Christ" is to know "living in Christ." The process entails putting off our "old self"—which is taking off those things that previously weighed us down, separated us from God, and held us back from living like Christ—and putting on the "new self"—which is essentially living like who we already are in Christ. By His grace that is at work within us, and with minds set on the Spirit, we are called to live into our true identity as children of God.

HOW DOES THIS EMPOWER MY PARENTING?

Let's talk about how this can become practical in our homes.

When our boys make poor choices and live outside of God's best, something we often say to them is, "Son, what you did is not who you are." We do this because it's important to help them understand that they are not the sum of their bad decisions—or their good ones, for that matter. We can say, "You lied, but that doesn't mean your identity is now a liar," or "You were terribly mean to your brother, but that doesn't mean your identity is now a terrible person. You aren't defined by what you do but by the God who created you. And He calls you an unconditionally loved son of God."

But there's more. We need to affirm that our children are made by God, on purpose, for a purpose, and we need to continually call our children up into living out their true identities with the help of the Holy Spirit. This might sound like us saying things like:

- "Remember who you are and Whose you are!"
- "I see what God has stored in you and how He is working through you to help others."
- "I see the great purpose on your life. I see who He is making you."
- "You get to participate in becoming more of who God made you to be by relying on the Spirit to help you walk faithfully."

We must encourage our children to become who they already are in Christ. (And if our children haven't professed Jesus as Lord, keep encouraging them in the good news of what Jesus did for them. Keep giving them the gospel. Keep teaching them about the free gift of eternal life and a new identity in Christ as a child of God!)

What language have you found helpful with your children when they make choices that aren't in alignment with who they are in Him and the way God has called them to live in obedience and abundance?

What changes might you need to make in your conversations that can help them live out their true identities as children of God?

In closing, let's make sure we know this and pass it on to our kids: Our sanctification—our growth in holiness—doesn't elevate our status before God. We can no more make Him like us with our godliness than we can make Him give up on us with our godlessness. We are covered in the complete righteousness of Christ when we first put our trust in Him. Rather, our pursuit of Christ is the proof that the Spirit is at work in our lives, purifying our desires and producing holiness in us for His glory.

DAY 4
HE PRODUCES FRUIT IN OUR LIVES

We are back in John 15 today to dive into how the Holy Spirit not only enables us to live fruitful lives but also the incredibly good news of how He produces fruit in our kids' lives.

> What does the Holy Spirit do in our kids lives, based on the sentence above?

Let's sit with that for a minute and do some honest inventory. This would have been an immensely helpful revelation for me when my kids were little and I thought that the responsibility of creating Christlike character in their lives was totally on me. And I've had enough conversations with other moms to know I wasn't alone in that false belief.

The message we mostly hear is that if we follow the right formulas and plant the right seeds, we will harvest the right fruit in our kids' lives. This leaves most Christian moms putting *so much pressure* on themselves to produce the fruit of the Spirit in their kids' lives.

When they're little, we might make charts that track their behavior and character. We may even add Bible verses to the chart that reinforce the fruit we are trying to cultivate. And when we see fruit in their lives we feel good about the kind of parents we are. And when we don't see the fruit, we feel like failures. It's so easy to believe that the burden of raising kids whose lives bear good fruit is entirely dependent on how well we till the soil and plant the seeds.

> Would you say this has been true of you? If so, describe the pressure this produces in your life. If not, describe the freedom the lack of pressure produces in your life.

Now hear me say that of course charts can be a helpful tool, and Bible verses are a vital way we train our kids. The Word of God is the most powerful means we have for raising our kids in righteousness, and we should utilize motivators and tools to help our littles learn. But these efforts on our part are not enough.

LIVING IN HIM

OPEN YOUR BIBLE and read Jesus' words in John 15:1-4.

Jesus is the vinedresser/gardener. How does He remain in us?

Can you see the work of the Father, the Son, and the Holy Spirit here? Isn't it glorious!

How does a branch bear fruit?

How do we bear fruit?

How, then, do our kids bear fruit?

How does this understanding change or reinforce the way in which you help your kids live fruit-bearing lives?

Now read verse 5.

Who is the vine? Who are the branches?

What happens if we remain in Him?

What happens apart from Him?

One of the things Jesus taught here is that while we might be productive people without entering into a relationship with Him, we won't be spiritually fruitful people—and there is a profound difference between the two.

Without the power of Christ working in us and through us, we are incapable of producing fruit that is God-glorifying. Even on our best days, filled with good works and good behavior, we know that our actions and motives are tainted with sin. We might have the desire to do what is right, but without the power of Christ, we can't execute. As Paul wrote in Romans 7:18,

> For I know that nothing good dwells in me, that is, in my flesh. For I have the desire to do what is right, but not the ability to carry it out.

Now read verses 6-8.

In this passage, Jesus wasn't describing Himself as genie that will grant us whatever we wish but as our God who invites us to align our hearts with His so our desires and prayers will line up with His desires for us and the world. When our longings and desires are oriented in Christ, all our asking will be fragranced by Christ and His desires for our lives.

Jesus closed by affirming what the fruit is meant to do.

In verse 8, for whose glory is our fruit?

For whose glory is our kids' fruit?

We need to know this! When our kids' lives produce fruit, it's not for our self-glorification. And when their lives don't produce fruit, it's not for our self-loathing. Mama, did you catch that? Goodness, I needed that.

Are you hard on yourself when it doesn't feel like your hard work is paying off? My hand is raised so high.

I'm not suggesting that we shouldn't be wholeheartedly committed to living lives that model the fruit of the Spirit to our kids and we shouldn't be equally committed to training our kids in righteousness. We should—100 percent. The difference is this: We need to know we are incapable of producing God-glorifying fruit in our lives apart from the Holy Spirit's power. And as we faithfully work to cultivate character in our kids' lives, we need to know we cannot control the outcome of our effort.

If we don't have time to make Jesus our top priority, our lives will never look like Jesus. If we think we are capable of becoming more like Jesus without abiding in Him, we'll fail every time.

And this lack of control over our kids only feels like bad news if we believe we are more capable than the Holy Spirit to create internal heart transformation. We cannot possibly care more about our kids living Christlike lives than their heavenly Father! Are you feelin' me? Now say this with me: *I will pursue Christ and the Spirit will produce Christlikeness in me.*

What will you do?

What will the Spirit do?

The fruit of the Spirit is the manifestation of the Holy Spirit's heart-work, not a parent's hard-work, in our kid's lives. It's why it's called the fruit of the Spirit, not the fruit of the parent. But if you only knew how often my hubby has to remind me that the Holy Spirit in our kids (or working to bring our kids to Christ) is where we need to keep our hope. I so quickly default to putting the onus back on me.

Now say this with me: *I will plant seeds in my kids' hearts and the Spirit will produce fruit in my kids' lives.*

What will you do?

What will the Spirit do?

Now that several of my boys are in their teens, and I've become even more aware of how powerless I am to force fruit in their lives, these are the truths I need to rehearse on the daily.

What worries have you been holding onto in your kids' lives that you need to surrender to God?

HOW DO I ABIDE?

When we are seeking to abide in God, we can make a deliberate effort to begin the day in dependence on Him and in relationship with Him. Welcome His presence. Ask for His power. Be aware of His provision. Be in continual communication with Him. Seek the Spirit's illumination as you spend time studying and meditating on God's Word. Invest time sitting in silence before Him to hear His voice. These spiritual disciplines—also known as "practicing His presence"— put us in a posture of receiving from His Spirit, like the life-giving sap of a vine, the nourishment required to produce the fruit. There is absolutely no substitute for it. This is how we pursue Christ.

Spiritual disciplines are the things that help strengthen our relationship with God and mature our faith:

- Bible study (2 Tim. 3:16)
- Prayer (Phil. 4:6)
- Worship (John 4:21-24)
- Fasting (Matt. 6:16-18)
- Giving (2 Cor. 9:6-8)
- Confession (1 John 1:9)
- Serving others (1 Pet. 4:10)
- Practicing gratitude and remembering what God has done (1 Thess. 5:18)
- Fellowship with other believers (Prov. 27:17)
- Sabbath rest and creating margin in your life (Deut. 5:12-15)

What disciplines stand out to you from the list above? Why?

How can practicing these spiritual disciplines help you as you seek to produce fruit in your life? In your parenting?

WHAT FRUIT DOES HE PRODUCE?

On Day 2 of this week we studied Galatians 5:16-17 and saw how vital it is for us to walk by the Spirit in our fight against the flesh. We're going to pick back up in verse 19 to wrap up the week.

OPEN YOUR BIBLE and read Galatians 5:19-24.

In the chart below, list the acts of the flesh (or, said differently, the fruit of self) in the left column. This is the fruit we produce apart from the Spirit. In the right column list the fruit of the Spirit, or what we gain from abiding in the Spirit.

Acts of the Flesh	Fruit of the Spirit

We don't have to stare at these two lists long to see the radical difference in what the self and the Spirit produce. When we operate in the power of self rather than in the power of the Spirit, our lives will manifest the fruit of self rather than the fruit of the Spirit. Thankfully, we now know that the fruit of the Spirit isn't a checklist of virtues we are expected to manufacture in our own power. It's the supernatural manifestation of a yielded heart abiding in Jesus.

Mama, you—and your children—are empowered to bear all the fruit when you abide in Him.

Is there specific fruit you've been trying to force but don't exhibit? Look again at the list Paul laid out and take a moment to pray and invite the Holy Spirit to become larger in your life so that His character—His fruit—will become what you bear!

The whole of the Christian life and the work of the Spirit of God is to bring glory to God. When we abide in Christ, the fruit is the proof, and the Father is praised. This is what the Holy Spirit does. He wants you and your children to flourish and thrive!

HOW DOES THIS EMPOWER MY PARENTING?

When it comes to planting seeds in our kids' hearts, we have God's Word, family prayer, Scripture memory, serving our neighbors, and worshiping in community. But let's not underestimate what happens in the simple conversations about Jesus in the car, on a walk, or at bedtime. Let's not underestimate the power of your kids watching you whisper a prayer for help when you're about to lose your patience or when you raise your voice in song as you worship to Christian music while you cook in the kitchen. The "big" and primary practices for planting seeds matter greatly, but don't get so overwhelmed by the big moments—when everyone is gathered around the table for a family devotion or serving at a soup kitchen—that you neglect to take advantage of the small in-betweens. Intentionally point out evidence of God's goodness in the mundane, act on the Spirit's nudging to be the love of Jesus to someone in need, or give grace to a kid who is struggling and needs to be reminded God never gives up on us or stops loving us.

Which practices for planting seeds comes most naturally for you? Why?

Do you sense the Spirit inviting you into a new practice for planting seeds? What is one step you can take today—big or small—to partner with the Spirit in producing fruit in your kids' lives?

#NeverAloneBibleStudy

THE GIFTS OF THE HOLY SPIRIT

In the seventh grade, while attending a private Christian school that was part of a large church, I wrote an essay about the gifts of the Holy Spirit for a class project. Looking back, I realize it would have been wise to ask my parents to read my essay before I submitted it. I was, after all, a Preacher's Kid, whose father led another large church in the area, so I had good reason to ask for their input, but I was at that stage where you think you know all things.

I honestly don't remember much about what I said in that essay, or even why I felt compelled to tackle such a topic at twelve years old, but I do remember it was written under the assumption that I knew far more than I actually did about spiritual gifts. That essay landed me a meeting with my teacher who was very gracious in helping me see how what I'd written revealed some holes in my understanding of the gifts the Holy Spirit gives.

You probably didn't write an essay on the gifts of the Holy Spirit, but maybe you resonate with having some holes in your understanding. Or perhaps you don't feel confused at all and you just long to learn more. Wherever you land, I am excited to share with you what I've learned since writing my not-so-stellar essay in middle school.

DAY 1
HE GIVES US SPIRITUAL GIFTS

In conversations about the Holy Spirit with women in varying walks of life, one thing has very much stood out to me: our exposure to and experience of (or lack of) spiritual gifts has mattered greatly in whether we've welcomed or avoided the Holy Spirit's manifestation in our lives.

For example, one friend's story especially stood out to me as she spoke of how she was raised in an environment that put immense pressure on congregants to exercise a particular gift and made them feel "less than" if they did not possess this gift. Another woman spoke of how her exposure to spiritual gifts at a young age was very positive, but it made her assume the Spirit's only relevance in her life was for gifting and not for daily empowerment for living.

> What experience (or lack thereof) have you had to the manifestation of the Spirit concerning spiritual gifts? How has this affected your openness to the Holy Spirit?

This can be a tricky conversation because there are so many misconceptions and myths about spiritual gifts. My goal is to open the Word of God and simply glean alongside you what the Spirit would teach us about Himself and the gifting He gives.

Paul generously gave us a great deal to glean about spiritual gifts that we can work out in our parenting. I've broken it down according to 1 Corinthians 12, our Scripture passage today, and I'm excited for us to discover this together.

OPEN YOUR BIBLE and read 1 Corinthians 12:1-11 to begin.

In verses 1-3, Paul explained that believers confess Jesus is Lord by the power of the Spirit. Since speech was likely the issue at hand in the church at Corinth, Paul proceeded with clarifying how believers exercise their spiritual gifts.

In verses 4-6, Paul wrote:

Now there are varieties of gifts, but the same Spirit; and there are varieties of service, but the same Lord; and there are varieties of activities, but it is the same God who empowers them all in everyone.

In the verses above, underline where you see each Person of the Trinity.

What is the significance of Paul making a trinitarian reference in his teaching?

The Father, Son, and Holy Spirit are inseparable. God is presently and actively at work as we exercise our gifts in the power of the Holy Spirit. Our gifts come from God and help us reflect His character, each working to build up the body of the church and bring others to salvation through Christ.

Now look at verse 7:

To each is given the manifestation of the Spirit for the common good.

We have some important things to glean here!

For what is every believer given the "manifestation of the Spirit?"

What does this mean for you as a believer?

Division occurs when we use our gifts for selfish gain and self-glorification. Our gifts serve a purpose, which is serving others. The gifts are about edification and are meant to bring unification, not division, which sadly happens often.

Knowing that the purpose of the gifts is to edify and unify, how can this change our posture about spiritual gifts if we are hesitant or fearful?

Some believers may be given more than one gift, but everyone is given at least one gift. The Holy Spirit chose your gift specifically for you. You have a significant role to play in the body of Christ. The Spirit also holds the authority to give different gifts at different times in your life. It's your responsibility to steward your gift well.

This is true for our believing children too! Think about that. What a beautiful message we get to pass onto our kids: "God has uniquely gifted you! And the gift God has given you is significant and essential for building up the church!"

Now let's discover what these extraordinary gifts are.

VARYING GIFTS

In verses 8-11 Paul identified nine gifts that come from one Spirit: (1) wisdom, (2) knowledge, (3) faith, (4) gifts of healings, (5) working of miracles, (6) prophecies, (7) distinguishing of spirits, (8) kinds of tongues, and (9) the interpretation of tongues. This list isn't exhaustive. In fact, Paul also listed gifts in Romans 12:6-8; Ephesians 4:11; and 1 Corinthians 12:28-31.

Do you know your spiritual gift(s)? Explain.

What gifts can you see demonstrated in your children?

Mama, you may already be flourishing in your gift, but if you don't know your gift yet, that is OK. That will be our discovery tomorrow when we take a survey to help us sort this out!

All of the gifts originate in and are empowered by God's Spirit, and everyone benefits from their manifestation. Paul's instruction to "pursue love, and earnestly desire the spiritual gifts" (1 Cor. 14:1) wasn't restricted to the early church. God still longs to manifest His Spirit in us, the church, today. Isn't that incredible? This is no small thing!

THE PURPOSE OF SPIRITUAL GIFTS
OPEN YOUR BIBLE and read 1 Corinthians 12:12-26.

What is the purpose of the body analogy Paul used here?

The gifts Paul mentioned all come from the same source—the divine Trinity—and the gifts are unified in their purpose:

> *The way God designed our bodies is a model for*
> *understanding our lives together as a church.*
> **1 CORINTHIANS 12:25, MSG**

My friend who felt "less than" or "left out" because she did not possess a certain spiritual gift is much like what was happening in the Corinthian church. They put so much importance on a certain gift, likely tongues, that those without it felt useless to the body of Christ.

GIFTS OF GRACE
The New Testament uses the Greek word *charisma* to speak of the spiritual gifts given to believers by the Holy Spirit. *Charisma* means "a gift of grace" and signifies a gracious work of God.[38] Spiritual gifts are a gracious work of God, just like the unearned and underserved love of God in Jesus Christ.

There are two additional things we should know about spiritual gifts. The first is that we don't get to choose our gifting. Unlike our children, who make lists of the gifts they'd like to be given on their birthdays, we don't get to pick out our spiritual gifts. No person, no matter how hard they want it or will it, can attain a spiritual gift that the Holy Spirit has not appointed. And here's the second thing. God won't retract our gift. That's a hard one to grasp. It would make more sense to the human mind if Scripture said God reserves the right to withdraw gifts based on how well we steward them. But grace is grace. It doesn't come with conditions.

Take a moment to reflect on the greatness of God's grace and His generosity to entrust you with a spiritual gift for His glory. He didn't have to do this; He chose to.

How do you feel about the spiritual gift (or gifts) God chose for you?

Have you wished you could choose a different gift or envied another's gift? If so, reflect on where that desire or envy stemmed from and explain it below.

I'll confess I have envied the spiritual gifts of certain spiritual giants in my life. I've wanted what they have. But I am humbled and led to repentance when I remember our gifts are given to serve others, not ourselves, and they are ultimately for God's exaltation, not our personal gain.

Paul wrote in 1 Corinthians 12:31,

> But earnestly desire the higher gifts.
> And I will show you a still more excellent way.

"Higher gifts" are those that bring the most benefit to the body of Christ rather than just to a single person. To "earnestly desire" the gifts is different from envying another person's gifts. This is about sincerely wanting everything the Spirit has to give you for the common good, and this includes your very own family.

Spiritual gifts are supernatural gifts, empowered by the Holy Spirit. These gifts exceed our human capacity. All of the gifts reveal God's power and all of the gifts are for God's glory. It's simply incredible that God enables us to experience His extraordinary power in our ordinary lives.

EXERCISING OUR GIFTS

When we turn the page in our Bibles to 1 Corinthians 13, we come to Paul's famous letter about love. We often hear this passage read at weddings and see its verses quoted in artwork. And while this is right and good, what we often miss is that Paul was writing about the utmost importance of love in exercising our spiritual gifts.

OPEN YOUR BIBLE and read 1 Corinthians 13:1-3.

Why is love an absolute necessity?

Love is essential in exercising our gifts, as our spiritual gifts can only be properly expressed through love. Said differently, the gifts of the Spirit must be carried out with the fruit of the Spirit. These incredible gifts are something God wants us to have and use and enjoy and grow *in love*.

I pray that in the church, and under our roofs, we can practice the gifts in love for the good of others and to the glory of the Father so we don't miss out on witnessing a mighty work of God in our midst.

HOW DOES THIS EMPOWER MY PARENTING?

We can draw much inspiration from this passage for our parenting, as it guides us in how we think about spiritual gifting in our homes. Meaning, the way God designed our bodies is a beautiful model for understanding how we are to function as families, exercise our gifts under our roofs, and serve one another in love. Each person in our families has diverse gifts. Each of us come together to form the body of the church, and all work together to accomplish unity, love, and to bring glory to God.

Based on the age of your child(ren), what is an important takeaway to teach them about what God has stored in them?

As moms, do we believe it's our duty to discuss this with our kids and introduce them to how the Spirit manifests Himself through us and our kids? Explain.

DAY 2
SPIRITUAL GIFTS SURVEY

Today will be a bit different than usual. We are going to use our time to take the Spiritual Gifts Survey and discover our unique gifting!

Before we begin, it's helpful to remember that any spiritual gifts survey isn't an absolute or perfect analysis. This is a tool intended to help you, but it's not a means to provide a definitive voice for how you're gifted. In fact, the best way to identify your gifting is within community. So we'll take the survey, but let's also talk to others. Ask them what they see in you or even let them take the survey for how they think you are equipped. Gifts for the church body are best discerned within the church body. We need one another!

DIRECTIONS

This is not a test, so there are no wrong answers. The Spiritual Gifts Survey consists of eighty statements. Some items reflect concrete actions, other items are descriptive traits, and still others are statements of belief.

- Select the response you feel best characterizes yourself, and place that number in the blank provided. Record your answer in the blank beside each item.
- Do not spend too much time on any one item. Remember, it is not a test. Usually your immediate response is best.
- Please give an answer for each item. Do not skip any items.
- Do not ask others how they are answering or how they think you should answer.
- Work at your own pace.

YOUR RESPONSE CHOICES ARE:

5—Highly characteristic of me/definitely true for me

4—Most of the time this would describe me/be true for me

3—Frequently characteristic of me/true for me—about 50 percent of the time

2—Occasionally characteristic of me/true for me—about 25 percent of the time

1—Not at all characteristic of me/definitely untrue for me

_____ 1. I have the ability to organize ideas, resources, time, and people effectively.

_____ 2. I am willing to study and prepare for the task of teaching.

_____ 3. I am able to relate the truths of God to specific situations.

_____ 4. I have a God-given ability to help others grow in their faith.

_____ 5. I possess a special ability to communicate the truth of salvation.

_____ 6. I have the ability to make critical decisions when necessary.

_____ 7. I am sensitive to the hurts of people.

_____ 8. I experience joy in meeting needs through sharing possessions.

_____ 9. I enjoy studying.

_____ 10. I have delivered God's message of warning and judgment.

_____ 11. I am able to sense the true motivation of persons and movements.

_____ 12. I have a special ability to trust God in difficult situations.

_____ 13. I have a strong desire to contribute to the establishment of new churches.

_____ 14. I take action to meet physical and practical needs rather than merely talking about or planning to help.

_____ 15. I enjoy entertaining guests in my home.

_____ 16. I can adapt my guidance to fit the maturity of those working with me.

_____ 17. I can delegate and assign meaningful work.

_____ 18. I have an ability and desire to teach.

_____ 19. I am usually able to analyze a situation correctly.

_____ 20. I have a natural tendency to encourage others.

_____ 21. I am willing to take the initiative in helping other Christians grow in their faith.

_____ 22. I have an acute awareness of the emotions of other people, such as loneliness, pain, fear, and anger.

_____ 23. I am a cheerful giver.

_____ 24. I spend time digging into facts.

_____ 25. I feel that I have a message from God to deliver to others.

_____ 26. I can recognize when a person is genuine/honest.

_____ 27. I am a person of vision (a clear mental portrait of a preferable future given by God). I am able to communicate vision in such a way that others commit to making the vision a reality.

_____ 28. I am willing to yield to God's will rather than question and waver.

_____ 29. I want to be more active in getting the gospel to people in other lands.

_____ 30. It makes me happy to do things for people in need.

_____ 31. I am successful in getting a group to do its work joyfully.

_____ 32. I am able to make strangers feel at ease.

_____ 33. I have the ability to plan learning approaches.

_____ 34. I can identify those who need encouragement.

_____ 35. I have trained Christians to be more obedient disciples of Christ.

_____ 36. I am willing to do whatever it takes to see others come to Christ.

_____ 37. I am attracted to people who are hurting.

_____ 38. I am a generous giver.

_____ 39. I am able to discover new truths.

_____ 40. I have spiritual insights from Scripture concerning issues and people that compel me to speak out.

_____ 41. I can sense when a person is acting in accord with God's will.

_____ 42. I can trust in God even when things look dark.

_____ 43. I can determine where God wants a group to go and help it get there.

_____ 44. I have a strong desire to take the gospel to places where it has never been heard.

_____ 45. I enjoy reaching out to new people in my church and community.

_____ 46. I am sensitive to the needs of people.

_____ 47. I have been able to make effective and efficient plans for accomplishing the goals of a group.

_____ 48. I often am consulted when fellow Christians are struggling to make difficult decisions.

_____ 49. I think about how I can comfort and encourage others in my congregation.

_____ 50. I am able to give spiritual direction to others.

_____ 51. I am able to present the gospel to lost persons in such a way that they accept the Lord and His salvation.

_____ 52. I possess an unusual capacity to understand the feelings of those in distress.

_____ 53. I have a strong sense of stewardship based on the recognition that God owns all things.

_____ 54. I have delivered to other persons messages that have come directly from God.

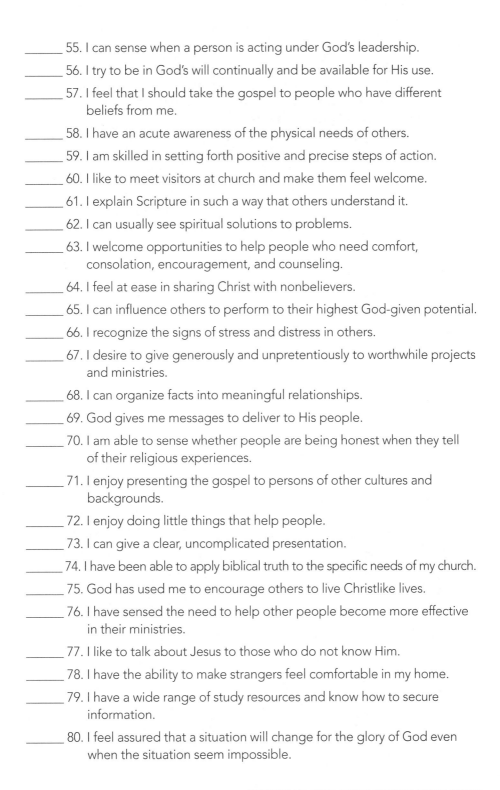

_____ 55. I can sense when a person is acting under God's leadership.

_____ 56. I try to be in God's will continually and be available for His use.

_____ 57. I feel that I should take the gospel to people who have different beliefs from me.

_____ 58. I have an acute awareness of the physical needs of others.

_____ 59. I am skilled in setting forth positive and precise steps of action.

_____ 60. I like to meet visitors at church and make them feel welcome.

_____ 61. I explain Scripture in such a way that others understand it.

_____ 62. I can usually see spiritual solutions to problems.

_____ 63. I welcome opportunities to help people who need comfort, consolation, encouragement, and counseling.

_____ 64. I feel at ease in sharing Christ with nonbelievers.

_____ 65. I can influence others to perform to their highest God-given potential.

_____ 66. I recognize the signs of stress and distress in others.

_____ 67. I desire to give generously and unpretentiously to worthwhile projects and ministries.

_____ 68. I can organize facts into meaningful relationships.

_____ 69. God gives me messages to deliver to His people.

_____ 70. I am able to sense whether people are being honest when they tell of their religious experiences.

_____ 71. I enjoy presenting the gospel to persons of other cultures and backgrounds.

_____ 72. I enjoy doing little things that help people.

_____ 73. I can give a clear, uncomplicated presentation.

_____ 74. I have been able to apply biblical truth to the specific needs of my church.

_____ 75. God has used me to encourage others to live Christlike lives.

_____ 76. I have sensed the need to help other people become more effective in their ministries.

_____ 77. I like to talk about Jesus to those who do not know Him.

_____ 78. I have the ability to make strangers feel comfortable in my home.

_____ 79. I have a wide range of study resources and know how to secure information.

_____ 80. I feel assured that a situation will change for the glory of God even when the situation seem impossible.

SCORING YOUR SURVEY

Follow these directions to compute your score for each spiritual gift.

1. Place in each box your numerical response (1-5) to the item number which is indicated below the box.
2. For each gift, add the numbers in the boxes and put the total in the TOTAL box.

LEADERSHIP	Q6 +	Q16 +	Q27 +	Q43 +	Q65 = TOTAL
ADMINISTRATION	Q1 +	Q17 +	Q31 +	Q47 +	Q59 = TOTAL
TEACHING	Q2 +	Q18 +	Q33 +	Q61 +	Q73 = TOTAL
KNOWLEDGE	Q9 +	Q24 +	Q39 +	Q68 +	Q79 = TOTAL
WISDOM	Q3 +	Q19 +	Q48 +	Q62 +	Q74 = TOTAL
PROPHECY	Q10 +	Q25 +	Q40 +	Q54 +	Q69 = TOTAL
DISCERNMENT	Q11 +	Q26 +	Q41 +	Q55 +	Q70 = TOTAL
EXHORTATION	Q20 +	Q34 +	Q49 +	Q63 +	Q75 = TOTAL
SHEPHERDING	Q4 +	Q21 +	Q35 +	Q50 +	Q76 = TOTAL
FAITH	Q12 +	Q28 +	Q42 +	Q56 +	Q80 = TOTAL
EVANGELISM	Q5 +	Q36 +	Q51 +	Q64 +	Q77 = TOTAL
APOSTLESHIP	Q13 +	Q29 +	Q44 +	Q57 +	Q71 = TOTAL
SERVICE/HELPS	Q14 +	Q30 +	Q46 +	Q58 +	Q72 = TOTAL
MERCY	Q7 +	Q22 +	Q37 +	Q52 +	Q66 = TOTAL
GIVING	Q8 +	Q23 +	Q38 +	Q53 +	Q67 = TOTAL
HOSPITALITY	Q15 +	Q32 +	Q45 +	Q60 +	Q78 = TOTAL

GRAPHING YOUR PROFILE

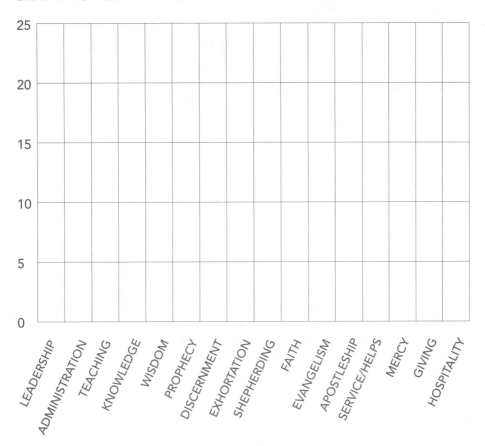

1. For each gift place a mark across the bar at the point that corresponds to your TOTAL for that gift.

2. For each gift shade the bar below the mark that you have drawn.

3. The resultant graph gives a picture of your gifts. Gifts for which the bars are tall are the ones in which you appear to be strongest. Gifts for which the bars are very short are the ones in which you appear not to be strong.

Now that you have completed the survey, I want to provide you with some things to think through in the weeks and months ahead.

The gifts I have begun to discover in my life are:

After prayer and worship, I am beginning to sense that God wants me to use my spiritual gifts to serve Christ's body by:

I am not sure yet how God wants me to use my gifts to serve others. But I am committed to prayer and worship, seeking wisdom and opportunities to use the gifts I have received from God.

Ask God to help you know how He has gifted you for service and how you can begin to use this gift in ministry to others, and this includes in your home.

How can the gift(s) you've begun to identify today impact your parenting or better equip you as a mom?

DAY 3
HE CAN BE QUENCHED

Now that we've gotten greater clarity on our spiritual gifts, we will continue in our conversation about the importance of putting those gifts to good use.

HOW WE QUENCH THE SPIRIT
OPEN YOUR BIBLE and read 1 Thessalonians 5:19-21.

What instruction did Paul give us in verse 19?

The ESV translates verse 19 as, "Do not quench the Spirit." According to *Strong's*, "quench" means "extinguish" or "suppress."[39] It likens our relationship with the Spirit to a fire that can be stifled to the point that it goes out. Sam Storms writes,

> *"The Spirit comes to us as a fire, either to be fanned into full flame and given the freedom to accomplish his will, or to be doused and extinguished by the water of human fear, control, and flawed theology. … The Holy Spirit wants to intensify the heat of his presence among us, to inflame our hearts and fill us with the warmth of his indwelling power."[40]*

But how do we know if we are releasing or restricting the Spirit? Quenching the Spirit is likely not something we intend to do, so how can we know? Paul answered that question in verses 20-21.

Fill in the blank with Paul's explanation:

"Do not despise _____, but test _____; hold fast _____."

Because the Holy Spirit has been abused and misused in the church, we have neglected His gifts and, in many ways, become fearful of His work. But as Paul taught, the answer to the misuse of a spiritual gift is not disuse. The answer is holding it up to Scripture and holding fast to what aligns.

Would you say this has been true of you? Have you been fearful of the manifestations of the Spirit? Or maybe you've been told that the gifts of the Spirit ceased to exist? Explain.

Rather than neglect this benefit of the Holy Spirit, we are to "test everything" (1 Thess. 5:21). But what exactly does that mean? Sam Storms, in his book *Understanding Spiritual Gifts*, says,

> *"They were to weigh, judge, evaluate, or assess what purports to be a prophetic word and then 'hold fast what is good' and 'abstain from every form of evil.' … How do we 'hold fast to what is good?' After careful analysis yields the conclusion that the utterance is most likely from the Spirit, we should embrace it, believe it, and obey whatever admonitions may be entailed by it."*[41]

Take a moment to ponder the following questions:

Am I restricting or releasing what the Spirit wants to do?

Have I extinguished the flame in my heart?

Have I suppressed His power in my home?

Have I resisted what He longs to do through me in my church?

As we consider fanning into flame the gifts God has given us, let us remember our gifts are meant to benefit the people in our own homes as much as they're meant to benefit the global church.

HOLY FIRE
Quenching the Spirit, however, is not restricted to spiritual gifts.

Holy fire is a symbol used throughout Scripture to describe the Holy Spirit. And a life that emanates the supernatural fire of the Spirit is available to every believer. Unfortunately, too many of us believe we are exempt from emanating His power, but I trust by now we know this to be untrue!

As Priscilla Shirer writes,

> *"Seeing holy fire in us is what will compel others to get off the fence of indifference and serve Him wholeheartedly. This is the unmistakable element that should differentiate our lives from all others. As the fire of God's Spirit falls afresh on us—gracing us with his favor, empowerment, fruit and gifts—our lives will be purpose-filled, glorifying to His name and bear eternal fruit. God's Spirit inspires, emboldens, sanctifies and stirs a holy fervor in the soul of a human, first at the moment of salvation and then ongoingly as the believer is molded into Jesus' image and continually impassioned to fulfill their divine purpose."*[42]

The fire of God's Spirit is what Paul wrote about in his second Letter to Timothy.

OPEN YOUR BIBLE and read 2 Timothy 1:6-7.

See, not only should we not extinguish the fire, we should actively seek to keep it burning—blazing, in fact!

Imagine this: You're gathered around the outdoor fire pit with your family on a cool fall evening. You're enjoying the glorious view of the lake, the warm drink in your hand, and the joy on your kids' faces as they squeeze the roasted marshmallows between two graham crackers and a slice of chocolate. But before long you begin to notice that the fire is beginning to flame out, and when it does, you'll lose the warmth of the fire and joy of the experience. What would you do? Let it die out or rekindle the embers? I'm going to guess you'd be intentional about fanning the flame.

Likewise, but to a much greater degree, we need to be intentional in fanning into flame the fire inside us. For the rest of our time today, let's see what Paul had to say about this.

A SPIRIT NOT OF FEAR
OPEN YOUR BIBLE and reread 2 Timothy 1:7.

Paul helps readers understand that the Holy Spirit is "a spirit not of fear." This is no small thing because most mamas know few things as well as we know fear. We have fear about the decisions our children are making, or will make, that impact their faith and their future. We have fear over the decisions we need to make on their behalf, whether that's medical decisions, schooling decisions, or even decisions around what freedoms to give them in everything from the friendships they invest in to the Internet they search. We fear for their physical safety and the eternal security of their souls. We fear we aren't doing enough and we fear we're doing too much.

What fears are you carrying today?

Lean in, my friend, because there is something God wants you to hear.

God's Spirit in you isn't a Spirit of fear. It's a Spirit of courage, calmness, and confidence. We can heed God's command to "not be afraid"—a command that is said to be given 365 times in the Bible—because the Spirit inside us gives us His courage, calmness, and confidence for what's before us and our kids.[43]

I don't mean to simplify the complexity of fear in our lives. There are very practical steps we must take and help we must get when our lives are paralyzed by fear. But I don't want us to neglect the Spirit's role in transforming us into people whose trust in God's faithfulness trumps our fear of the unknown. For whatever fears you named, speak this over them: "God in me is not afraid, so neither shall I be, by the power of the Holy Spirit."

Let me share a personal story with you. Growing up, I had an immense amount of fear about my safety. I had terrible thoughts about what could happen to me when I wasn't alert or on guard. This carried into my adulthood and even my motherhood. I feared greatly for my children's safety. My husband often traveled for work after we had our first son, Cal. Setting the security alarm at night was only one of many steps I took in an attempt to ensure our safety and soothe my fears. And while I may have ensured our safety, my fear never really stilled. My spirit of fear was all-consuming when my husband wasn't home. My mom would often come to visit me when Mike was traveling to lend a hand and enjoy her grandson, and she began to see firsthand how my fear was worsening. In her infinite wisdom, she wrote out a list of Bible verses for me to pray over my fear and left the list with me when she returned home to my Dad.

That night, after I put my son to sleep and climbed into bed, I opened my Bible to look up the verses she gave me. One of the first verses on the list was Proverbs 3:5-6. She wrote it using the abbreviation "Pr. 3:5-6." I have perfect vision so I should have read it correctly, but instead I read "Ps. 3:5-6."

When I opened my Bible to the passage, I quickly realized that not only did I misread what my mom wrote down for me but God had appointed this moment to set me free.

Psalm 3:5-6 reads,

> *I lay down and slept; I woke again, for the LORD*
> *sustained me. I will not be afraid of many thousands of*
> *people who have set themselves against me all around.*

I read it over and over again through tear-drenched eyes, then slid my finger to verse 1 so I could read the whole chapter, only to become even more undone.

Psalm 3:3-4 says,

> *But you, O LORD, are a shield about me, my glory,*
> *and the lifter of my head. I cried aloud to the LORD,*
> *and he answered me from his holy hill.*

The Holy Spirit led me straight to truth that supernaturally set me free from fear, and I was never the same.

This is the work the Spirit wants to do in each one of us. He wants to work supernaturally to help us break through what seems like immovable barriers to living free from fear. He wants to empower us to live in the assurance that "the one who is in [us] is greater than the one who is in the world" (1 John 4:4, NIV).

Reading Psalm 3 was, of course, one of those "big moments," so I also want to encourage us for the small, daily moments of our motherhood that usually won't look like this. His Spirit is still very much present and moving in power.

> Take a moment to pray and surrender the fears you recorded to God. Ask Him to make His Spirit of power, love, and self-control very real to you right now. Give Him your fear and ask Him to fill that space with the warmth of His indwelling presence and the assurance of His indwelling power.

A SPIRIT OF POWER
The Spirit of power Paul wrote about in 2 Timothy 1:7 is not our spirit; it's the gifting of the Holy Spirit. This power isn't a force we wield but a Person to whom we yield. The Greek word for power in this verse is *dunamis*, from which we get

the words *dynamite* and *dynamic*.[44] This is extraordinary power that produces vibrant followers of Jesus (Rom. 15:13).

We can work up the willpower to change but it will only get us so far. The truth is, we don't need more willpower; we need more Spirit-power.

Are you struggling in your marriage? Are you overwhelmed and defeated in your parenting? Are you in the midst of making a big decision about your future, or are you pursuing a dream in your heart? Do you need help navigating a career choice or direction in fixing your finances? Does your relationship with God feel stale? Are you fighting the same old strongholds, or is shame crushing your spirit?

If there is fruit you wish to see in your life but don't, if there is victory over sin you wish you had but don't, run to the Spirit of power. He is for you, and He is for now.

Describe the difference in willpower and Spirit-power.

How can you experience more Spirit-generated power in your life today? Explain.

A SPIRIT OF LOVE
God is love, and the Holy Spirit is the bond of love between the Father and the Son. (Isn't that so beautiful?)

OPEN YOUR BIBLE and read John 13:34-35.

What was the new commandment Jesus gave to His disciples?

How did Jesus say people will know we are His disciples?

The kind of love Jesus calls for is only possible through the Spirit of love. It's Spirit-generated love that points others to Jesus' sacrificial love.

As parents, we love our kids wildly and wholeheartedly. But only God loves with a perfect love. An utterly unwavering and unconditional love. And we need Him to infuse our hearts with this love. May our prayer be that our kids know more of God's love because they witness it in us and experience a glimpse of it through us. May we be so filled with His grace that it can't help but overflow into our parenting. This Spirit-generated love is how the gospel becomes contagious in our homes.

> What circumstances or weaknesses in your kids tempt you to withhold love?

It is precisely in these times when you can call on the Spirit of love to manifest Himself in you.

> Let's spend a moment inviting the Holy Spirit to do that now— to invade our spirit with God's perfect love for our children.

The only way to have greater love flow from our lives is to ask the Holy Spirit to become larger in our lives. When the Holy Spirit is large in our lives, He's pointing us to Jesus and exalting the incarnate Son. We need Him to flood every room in our hearts so His love will overflow into every room in our homes.

A SPIRIT OF SELF-CONTROL

I take great encouragement knowing that the Holy Spirit in me is able to produce self-control from me. If you've read my previous study you already know that self-control, particularly in my role as a mom, is something I've needed God to supernaturally create in me. I never knew how angry I could get—or how loud I could yell—until I became a mom. This is the secret shame so many parents carry.

> What situations in your parenting tempt you to lose self-control?

Just this morning I lost my self-control. The boys' verbal arguing boiled over into physical fighting, and I let them know how I felt about it in no uncertain terms. But I didn't exercise my anger in the Spirit (capital S) of self-control. I exercised it in the spirit (lowercase s) of self-control. In other words, I exercised my anger in the flesh. I didn't yield, so I made matters worse. Which led to not only my children needing to seek forgiveness for their sin, but led to me needing to seek forgiveness for mine. I could justify how I responded by saying I can only take so much, and that is true. I can only take so much. But the Spirit of self-control is inexhaustible. It's why we need Him. He can take it all.

> Jesus used the Word to defeat Satan's temptation to sin in the desert (see Luke 4). We can commit to doing the same. What if we commit 2 Timothy 1:7 to memory and recite it aloud when our self-control is tested? Identify a practical way you can begin to practice this today.

Having the Spirit of self-control inside me assures me I have been enabled to choose gentleness and kindness in my words and tone, which I can exercise when I am yielded to Him.

This is not feel-good fluff. This is the real stuff, and it's changing me. Have I arrived? Obviously not. It's a process that the Spirit will continue and "bring it to completion" when Jesus returns (Phil. 1:6). But growth is happening, even on days like today when the enemy whispers, *Shame on you for writing about the Spirit of self-control when your actions today didn't witness to it.* He knows our tender spots, and he goes right for them. But when his voice of condemnation tries to attack we can quiet it with the voice of the Advocate, affirming, *God will never give up on you!*

Maybe you need the Holy Spirit's supernatural self-control to be victorious over an addiction or secret sin or something you run to in order to numb. We all have something, because we're human! The question is, do we live powerless under it or victorious over it?

Identify the areas in your life—or specifically parenting—where you need the Spirit of self-control in your life. Are you willing to yield so He can work out His self-control in your life?

Our struggles are no match for the Holy Spirit's uncontainable power. He wants to help us live in the freedom for which Christ has set us free! When the Spirit indwells us, He unites us to the Son, and our humanity is "born again"—or made new in Him. So that now, we have Christ's new humanity. He wants to give us self-control in every circumstance where we feel out of control. Because when we grow in self-control (among other habits), we are growing in Christlikeness. We are living out the reality of our newness in Christ and growing into maturity in Him.

But we have to cooperate. We must surrender ourselves and do what He calls us to do. It requires turning from self and toward God. And in doing so, His holy fire will emanate from within. Fan the flame within, friend!

HOW DOES THIS EMPOWER MY PARENTING?
Take a moment to further reflect on how 2 Timothy 1:7 is good news for your kids.

When they see you freed from fears that have held you hostage, what hope can that instill in them?

When they experience unconditional love in moments of unlovability, how can this draw them deeper into the Spirit of love?

When they see you yielding to the Spirit of self-control, what does that teach them about what's possible for them?

DAY 4
HE HELPS US LIVE IN FREEDOM

In the early days of our study, I mentioned how revelatory it was for me to recognize that although I'd been set free by Jesus, I'd been trying to stay free in my own strength. I didn't grasp or appreciate the extraordinary news of the Holy Spirit's power to help me live out the freedom Jesus secured for me. So as we wrap up these incredible seven weeks together, it feels fitting that we celebrate how far we've come in not only understanding, but experiencing the incredible freedom the Spirit carries out in the Christian life.

OPEN YOUR BIBLE and read Galatians 5:1.

For what did Jesus set us free?

Of what did Paul warn us?

We know that when Jesus finished the work He was sent to do through His death on the cross, He set us free. He secured our freedom from gaining God's favor through perfect obedience to the law, freedom from sin's dominion over our lives, and freedom from condemnation and shame.

Jesus was the only One who can (and did!) fulfill the rigorous demands of the law, securing God's eternal favor for us (1 Pet. 1:18-19). Real freedom is knowing that the perfection of Jesus covering us is what makes us pleasing to God.

Have you feared that God's pleasure in you is dependent on the progress you make toward perfection? Have you worried you will lose God's love when you don't meet the demands of the law?

If so, how did that fear and worry impact your relationship with God, or how is it impacting it now?

If not, how has your confidence in being covered by the righteousness of Christ impacted your relationship with God?

Here is something to think about for our parenting: When we are not living under God's grace, it's impossible to lead with God's grace. When we live under the pressure of the law, we will likely parent our children with the same pressure, and we will impede their understanding of the unconditional love of God. I speak from experience on this one.

I spent too many years trying to keep God happy by trying to keep a clean heart. I didn't know that what He really wanted was for me to seek His heart—and in doing so, the Spirit would sanctify mine.

He has given us a new heart—Christ's heart.

> *I have been crucified with Christ. It is no longer I who live,*
> *but Christ who lives in me. And the life I now live in the flesh I live*
> *by faith in the Son of God, who loved me and gave himself for me.*
> GALATIANS 2:20

It's not just that Jesus fulfilled the law and so His righteousness is accredited to us, as if it were separate from Him. We have His righteous because we are in Him. If we sit with that, how can it not take our breath away?

Because I didn't grasp the Spirit's role in helping me live out my freedom in Christ, I was a mom who was more focused on getting my little kids to obey perfectly than I was on giving them the good news of how Jesus obeyed perfectly on their behalf. I was giving them God's good and life-giving commands, but I wasn't weaving grace into how I instructed and disciplined them. I wasn't parenting in the freedom for which Christ has set us free.

In what ways do you see your freedom (or lack thereof) weaving its way into your parenting?

FREEDOM TO LIVE IN HIS IMAGE

When Paul wrote about freedom, we of course know that he never meant that we are free to do as we please. He meant we are free to do what pleases God. We are free to live in agreement with our identity as children of God in Christ through the life-giving Spirit.

The Holy Spirit carries out the freedom that we have in Christ! The Spirit unites us to the renewed humanity of the Son, and exercising our Christian freedom forms us into the image of the Son.

Jesus purchased our freedom on the cross with His blood. The Spirit puts it into full operation in our lives with His power!

Who purchased our freedom?

Who puts it into full operation in our lives?

OPEN YOUR BIBLE and read Romans 8:1-6.

In verses 1-4, Paul explained that the "Spirit of life"—the Holy Spirit—plays an active role in our freedom over sin's dominant power in our lives. As believers, we don't live under the control of our flesh but in the power of the Spirit.

Now watch what Paul did.

In verses 5-6, Paul showed us how "according to the flesh" and "according to the Spirit" are two mutually exclusive ways of life. Its purpose is to show us very plainly what we are given as people of the Spirit.

What did Paul say setting our minds on the flesh leads to?
(Remember, our flesh is our sinful human nature.)

What did he say setting our minds on the Spirit leads to?

To set our minds on the flesh is to desire and pursue sin. To set our minds on the Spirit is to desire and pursue holiness. Sadly, I think holiness gets a bad rap. We should talk about that for a second, because too many of us equate holiness with the try-hard life, which makes us spiritually tired. Or we reject the pursuit of holiness because we assume it leads to boredom.

Seriously, the enemy has done a marvelous job at making holiness, which is the defining characteristic of God, present as an exhausting, joyless pursuit. So instead of submitting ourselves to the often messy but always miraculous process of sanctification, we seek satisfaction outside of where the Spirit leads us. We forfeit the life and peace that Jesus came and died and rose again to give us.

The lie the enemy feeds us stands in stark contrast to what Jesus actually did:

I came so they can have real and eternal life,
more and better life than they ever dreamed of.
JOHN 10:10, THE MESSAGE

The Holy Spirit is the One who gives us power for the "more and better than we ever dreamed of" life! But we also play a vital role in this process. To "set our minds" means to make a choice. It doesn't just happen.

On what are you setting your mind in the morning?

In the middle of the day?

When you collapse into bed?

When you wake in the middle of the night?

Let us resolve not to forfeit the life and peace the Spirit applies to our hearts and minds. It was bought at the highest price—with our precious Savior's life.

FIGHT THE GOOD FIGHT

When Satan tempts you to believe that your sinful nature still holds authority over you, remind him whose power resides inside you. The Spirit of Almighty God! Through the indwelling Holy Spirit, you have the supernatural power to defeat the enemy's temptation. You have a renewed humanity, a new nature in Christ. Victory is yours in Jesus' name.

We are fighting a battle that has already been won! Do our kids know this? Do we talk about this? The power of the Spirt at work inside them is greater than the pull of sin at work against them.

OPEN YOUR BIBLE and read 1 John 4:4 (NLT).

Fill in the blanks below.

"But you belong to God, my dear children. You have already won a victory over those people, because the Spirit _____

_____ ."

This is incredibly good news for a teenager battling temptation or even a young child throwing a tantrum.

Below are a couple ways you might start the conversation with your children and then Scripture you can use to help them pray over their situation. They can personalize these prayers to welcome the Spirit's help in their struggles.

- "Son, you don't have to fight your temptation to _____ in your own strength. Because you have put your trust in Jesus, you have the Holy Spirit who was given to help you make wise choices that are for your good. You get to be strong in the Spirit's power!"

- "Finally, be strong in the Lord and in the strength of his might. Put on the whole armor of God, that you may be able to stand against the schemes of the devil. For we do not wrestle against flesh and blood, but against the rulers, against the authorities, against the cosmic powers over this present darkness, against the spiritual forces of evil in the heavenly places" (Eph. 6:10-12).

- "Daughter, when you get angry, call on the Holy Spirit in you so you don't sin in your anger. He can give you the self-control you want to have but can't come up with on your own. It's OK to feel angry, but don't let your anger win. Let the Spirit help you."

- "Don't sin by letting anger control you" (Eph. 4:26, NLT).

- "For God gave us a spirit not of fear but of power and love and self-control" (2 Tim. 1:7).

What messaging would you add to this list to help your kids set their minds on the Spirit? If you're studying in a group, these examples can be super helpful to other moms. Encourage each other with words God has given you to speak over your kids!

Those who belong to God and have the Holy Spirit have already won the victory. Are we teaching our kids to live in that victory? Of course, to teach and model victory requires us knowing and living it first. (This obviously isn't something we can or will do perfectly or all the time. There is grace here! But are we being intentional in allowing our kids to witness the power of the Holy Spirit in us?)

Where do you need a breakthrough? By the same power that fell down in the upper room, we can walk in victory today!

If you're holding this Bible study in your hands, then there's one thing I can assuredly say about you: You long to be a really good mom and you long to live out the freedom Jesus secured for you. I do too.

Identify a few ways you plan to be intentional in setting your mind on the Spirit and living out your freedom in Christ.

The Spirit wants to manifest His power in your life to help you grow in the likeness of Christ. He wants your children to know what's possible with Him through what they witness in you!

What a privilege it is to model the Spirit's power to our kids!

He wants our stories to testify to the unlimited benefits given through the Holy Spirit. Will we let Him?

FIND FREEDOM
OPEN YOUR BIBLE and read 2 Corinthians 3:17.

Write this verse below.

We could actually spend an entire day of study unpacking this verse, but there is one thing we must celebrate before we close: Where the Spirit is, freedom is!

What Paul emphasized is that the freedom that comes through salvation in Jesus and the indwelling Person of the Holy Spirit is deep and wide. The indwelling of the Spirit unites us to the Son, and this applies to every aspect of our lives.

- It's freedom from condemnation and shame.
- It's freedom from strongholds of our minds—the lethal lies and toxic thoughts that take up residence and seek to destroy us.
- It's freedom from slavery to sin and addiction.
- It's freedom from being controlled by worry and fear and anger and resentment.
- It's freedom from striving to attain an unattainable righteousness.
- It's freedom to enjoy life and peace and to lead our children in doing the same!

Where do you need the Spirit to apply the freedom that Jesus bought?

Don't hold back out of fear of disappointment. Because here's the truth: There is power in the mighty name of Jesus, and He has already won the victory. Be ready to see Him move in your life and your family.

HOW DOES THIS EMPOWER MY PARENTING?

Mama, Jesus set you free. Now the Spirit is in you to help you live free and parent free.

> In closing, I'd encourage you to return to Ephesians 1 and read it in light of everything we've learned. Will you do that now?

Now let's personalize this passage to help us end our time together in prayer!

So we praise God for the glorious grace He has poured out on us who belong to His dear Son. He is so rich in kindness and grace that He purchased our freedom with the blood of His Son and forgave our sins (vv. 6-7).

And when I believed in Christ, He identified me as His own by giving me the Holy Spirit, whom He promised long ago. The Spirit is God's guarantee that He will give me the inheritance He promised and that He has purchased me to be His own. He did this so I would praise and glorify Him (vv. 13-14).

I pray that my heart will be flooded with light so that I can understand the confident hope He has given to those He called—His holy people who are His rich and glorious inheritance. I also pray that I will understand the incredible greatness of God's power for me because I believe Him (vv. 18-19).

In Jesus' mighty name, Amen.

We said it on the very first day of our study, and it's time to say it again: "I am anointed by the Holy Spirit!"

Mama, we are Spirit-people! Everything we need to parent the children God has entrusted to us is already inside us through His Spirit. We get to parent in the power of the Holy Spirit!

So come, Holy Spirit! Awaken us to Your presence and power! Flood our hearts and homes, and transform us and our children into the image of our King Jesus, for the glory of the Father! Amen!

LEADER GUIDE

OPTIONAL INTRODUCTORY SESSION

Welcome moms to the Introductory Session of *Never Alone*. Provide name tags, and distribute Bible study books. Ask moms to share the names and ages of their children and why they were drawn to this Bible study. Give a short overview of the study, sharing the session titles and how there is personal study for them to do each week. Encourage moms to do what they can. If they are unable to complete all four days of the personal study, they can still learn and contribute in the group time each week. Help moms brainstorm specific times when they might try to complete their personal study each day. Use these questions as a way to introduce your group to one another.

- What are the best parts of parenting for you? What are the hardest parts?
- Name some common parenting struggles and concerns. How would you encourage a close friend who is worried about these situations?
- When do you feel most alone in your parenting?
- What role does the Holy Spirit currently play in your life?
- What do you want to gain most from this Bible study and this group?
- How can the group pray for you?

Close with prayer.

SESSION 1: THE PRESENCE OF THE HOLY SPIRIT

Welcome moms to Session 1 of *Never Alone*. Allow introductions for any newcomers. Invite women to share one crazy mom story in pairs. Then use these questions to review the first week's personal study.

- What was the most meaningful or significant thing you learned from the first week's personal study?
- Right or wrong, what beliefs do you currently have about the Holy Spirit?
- How is the Holy Spirit to a believer's advantage?
- What has prevented you from pursuing the Spirit in a more intimate way?
- In what ways have you seen the Spirit help you in the seasons of life—the ups and downs, the dull and the flourishing?
- How have you seen God turn your shortcomings into strengths in your parenting?
- Review the roles the Holy Spirit plays on page 18. How do these benefits of the Spirit bring you confidence and hope for the future?
- What are some ways we can connect with the Spirit in the midst of the daily routines of motherhood?
- What situations are your children currently facing where they need to know they have the Holy Spirit to help them and empower them?

Close in a time of silent prayer. Ask women to pray specifically for their children.

SESSION 2: THE PERSON OF THE HOLY SPIRIT

Welcome your group to Session 2 of *Never Alone*. Distribute strips of paper and ask women to write down one question about parenting in the Spirit they are grappling with. Invite volunteers to share their responses with the group. Use the following questions to review last week's personal study.

- How did God speak to you most through last week's study?
- What helps you cope when you feel overwhelmed with parenting? How have others encouraged you during those situations?
- How much pressure do you feel to hold all things together for your children when it feels like it's all falling apart? What are the consequences of trying to be the perfect example for our kids to follow?
- How is striving to be a flawless example different than seeking to live in pursuit of Christ by the power of the Holy Spirit?
- What does it mean to rely on the Spirit's power? How would relying on the Spirit change your parenting?
- What is the greatest way we can encourage one another to lean on the Spirit's power?
- What are some ways we can cultivate grace-filled responses to our children's disobedience?
- What fears did God ask you to lay aside during this week's study?
- How can mamas create opportunities to weave the good news of having the Holy Spirit into everyday conversation? Take a moment to pray for those children who haven't yet come to Christ. Ask that God would continue to draw them to Himself.

Direct women to pray in small groups. Encourage them to pray for one another and their children, trusting in God's power, promises, and plans.

SESSION 3: THE POWER OF THE HOLY SPIRIT

Welcome moms to Session 3 of *Never Alone*. Encourage women to share ways they've seen prayers answered since the beginning of the study. Use the following questions to review last week's personal study.

- What was the most meaningful or significant thing you learned from last week's study?
- Read John 14:16-31. How did Jesus prepare His disciples for the coming Holy Spirit? Do you struggle with believing the Holy Spirit equips you with the same power He gave to His disciples? Explain.
- What are some parenting decisions you're wading through right now?
- What would relying on the power of the Spirit look like in those decisions?
- What are some ways we can talk with our children about the power of the Holy Spirit no matter their age?
- How can we become more reliant on the Spirit—and less on ourselves—in our parenting?
- How can we more regularly incorporate prayer into our time with our children?
- What fruit of the Spirit is displayed well in your home? What fruit of the Spirit needs more development?

- What's something you know you can't do on your own and need the Spirit's power to achieve?

Pray for the moms, asking for full faith that God will lavishly provide His Spirit as we boldly guide our children to follow Jesus.

SESSION 4: THE LEADERSHIP OF THE HOLY SPIRIT

Welcome moms to Session 4 of *Never Alone*. Use these additional questions to review last week's personal study.

- What most resonated with you as a mom from last week's study?
- Based on this week's study, what does it mean to live filled with the Spirit?
- In what ways do you model confession and repentance for your children?
- In what ways are you cultivating your relationship with God?
- How does knowing what the Holy Spirit wants to do for you encourage you as you consider your calling to give your kids the gospel?
- What have you learned about the Spirit's essential role in knowing God as a relational and trustworthy Father?
- Share a time when you sensed God's love and comfort during suffering or sadness. How did you know this was the supernatural work of the Holy Spirit?
- Share a time when Scripture specifically spoke to your parenting.
- What steps with the Spirit of truth did you identify to silence the enemy?

- What changes have you made in your parenting as a result of meeting with this group and doing this Bible study?

Close with prayer and encourage women to text, email, or call another mom this week and affirm the transformation they see in her.

SESSION 5: THE CHAMPIONING OF THE HOLY SPIRIT

Welcome moms to Session 5 of *Never Alone*. Use these questions to review last week's personal study.

- When have you seen a difference in another mom and her parenting because of her relationship with Christ and walking with Him daily?
- What was the most meaningful or significant thing you learned from last week's study?
- What was your experience like with rules and obedience growing up?
- How have you seen other parents discipling their children that encouraged you?
- What bubbles up inside of you when you think about the Holy Spirit championing you or your child?
- Share a time when you felt the nudge of the Spirit and obeyed what He was telling you to do (or not to do).
- How can parents cultivate the fruit of the Spirit in their children?
- What is one step you can take today— big or small—to partner with the Spirit in producing fruit in your kids' lives?
- When have you experienced God's power in your weakness? When has

your weakness allowed margin to see God at work in your life?

- Based on this week's study, what do you want to quit doing? What is important to begin doing?
- Review the bulleted list on page 149 of our identity in Christ. What emotions do these facts bring to mind?

Pray for the moms and let them know you are available to talk and pray after the session if they have special prayer needs.

SESSION 6: THE SANCTIFYING OF THE HOLY SPIRIT

Welcome moms to Session 6 of *Never Alone*. Use these questions to review last week's personal study.

- In what ways do you model growing closer to God?
- How do you reconcile knowing you will mess up with your kids with the knowledge that God chose you to be their mama?
- How can we partner with the Holy Spirit in helping our kids know their righteousness is in Jesus alone?
- What fears do moms have about relying on the grace of the gospel to do what God's Word says He will do?
- What things do you want most for your children?
- Evaluate your life—time, money, energy, focus. What changes need to be made to better prioritize the things you desire for your kids? How would living this way change the way you parent?

Close in prayer and encourage moms to complete their final week of homework before the last group session.

SESSION 7: THE GIFTS OF THE HOLY SPIRIT AND WRAP-UP

Welcome moms to the final group time, Session 7 of *Never Alone*.

- What did the spiritual gifts test reveal to you?
- What gifts have other people identified in you? What gifts have you seen in your children?
- What words, phrases, and actions can you use at home to encourage your children to develop their giftings?
- What keeps you from utilizing your gifts more?
- Review the session titles of *Never Alone* and identify one truth you learned from each week. What will you do to take the truths you've learned and incorporate them into your life and your parenting?
- What tools has this study given you as you lean into the Holy Spirit's power for your parenting?

Close in prayer that the group will remember the truths they have learned in this study and will rely on the Holy Spirit for their parenting.

ENDNOTES

1. *The Baptist Faith & Message* (2000 Tract).
2. "Parakletos," Strong's G3875, *Blue Letter Bible* online. Available at www.blueletterbible.org.
3. R. Kent Hughes, *John: That You May Believe, Preaching the Word* (Wheaton, IL: Crossway Books, 1999), 342–344.
4. Billy Graham, *The Holy Spirit: Activating God's Power in Your Life* (Nashville, TN: Thomas Nelson, 1978), 32.
5. "Doxazō," Strong's G1392, *Blue Letter Bible* online. Available at www.blueletterbible.org.
6. Sinclair B. Ferguson, *The Holy Spirit* (Downers Grove, IL: InterVarsity, 1996), 21.
7. Millard Erickson, Christian Theology (Ada, MI: Baker Academic, 2013), 363.
8. "Trinity," *Holman Bible Dictionary* (Nashville, TN: Holman Bible Publishers, 1991), 1372.
9. *Christian Theology*, 875-876.
10. "Lupeo," Strong's G3076. *Blue Letter Bible* online. Available at www.blueletterbible.org.
11. *ESV Gospel Transformation Bible, Commentary on Matthew* 12:31–32, (Wheaton, IL: Crossway, 2011), 1287.
12. Max Anders and Stuart K. Weber, *Matthew: Holman New Testament Commentary*, vol. 1 (Nashville, TN: B&H Publishing Group, 2012).
13. Corrie ten Boom, *Tramp for the Lord: The Story that Begins Where The Hiding Place Ends* (Fort Washington, PA: CLC Publications, 1974), 63.
14. "Plēroō," Strong's G4137, *Blue Letter Bible* online. Available at www.blueletterbible.org.
15. J. Goetzmann, "*metanoia*," ed. Lothar Coenen, Erich Beyreuther, and Hans Bietenhard, *New International Dictionary of New Testament Theology* (Grand Rapids, MI: Zondervan Publishing House, 1986), 357.
16. John Piper, "How to Seek the Holy Spirit," DesiringGod.org, January 15, 2018, https://www.desiringgod.org/messages/how-to-seek-the-holy-spirit.
17. Peter H. Davids, *The Letters of 2 Peter and Jude, The Pillar New Testament Commentary* (Grand Rapids, MI: William B. Eerdmans, 2006), 210.
18. "Energēs," Strong's G1756, *Blue Letter Bible* online. Available at www.blueletterbible.org.
19. "Doxazō," Strong's G1392, *Blue Letter Bible* online. Available at www.blueletterbible.org.
20. Holy Cross Greek Orthodox Church, "The Nicene Creed," https://www.holycrosspgh.org/nicene-creed, accessed July 20, 2021.
21. John Piper, "God Will Give You Something to Say," DesiringGod.org, December 27, 2016, https://www.desiringgod.org/articles/god-will-give-you-something-to-say
22. "Champion," YourDictionary.com, https://www.yourdictionary.com/champion, accessed July 15, 2021.
23. Glenn Stanton, "FactChecker: Does 'Abba' Mean 'Daddy'?", TheGospelCoalition.org, May 13, 2013, https://www.thegospelcoalition.org/article/factchecker-does-abba-mean-daddy/.
24. Tim Keller, *Prayer: Experiencing Awe and Intimacy with God* (New York, NY: Penguin Books, 2016), 172–173.
25. John Piper, "The Love of God Has Been Poured Out Within Our Hearts," DesiringGod.org, November 28, 1999, https://www.desiringgod.org/messages/the-love-of-god-has-been-poured-out-within-our-hearts.
26. *ESV Gospel Transformation Bible*, 1507.
27. John Piper, "What Is Hope?", DesiringGod.org, April 6, 1986, https://www.desiringgod.org/messages/what-is-hope.
28. *Prayer: Experiencing Awe and Intimacy with God.*
29. Jodie Berndt, *Praying the Scriptures for Your Teens* (Grand Rapids, MI: Zondervan, 2007).
30. "Parakletos," Strong's G3875, *Blue Letter Bible* online. Available at www.blueletterbible.org.
31. "Self-help," Merriam-Webster.com, https://www.merriam-webster.com/dictionary/self-help, accessed July 17, 2021.
32. James Beevers, "Do You Love Yourself Enough?", DesiringGod.org, January 11, 2017, https://www.desiringgod.org/articles/do-you-love-yourself-enough
33. William Arndt et al., *A Greek-English Lexicon of the New Testament and Other Early Christian Literature* (Chicago, IL: University of Chicago Press, 2000), 315.
34. John Piper, "Jesus Is Precious Because We Yearn for Beauty", DesiringGod.org, March 28, 1982, https://www.desiringgod.org/messages/jesus-is-precious-because-we-yearn-for-beauty.
35. "Pneuma," Strong's G4151, *Blue Letter Bible* online. Available at www.blueletterbible.org.
36. "hagiazó," Strong's Concordance, Bible Hub, Biblehub.com, https://biblehub.com/greek/38.htm
37. Max Anders, *Galatians, Ephesians, Philippians & Colossians, Holman New Testament Commentary*, vol. 8 (Nashville, TN: B&H Publishing Group, 2012).
38. James Swanson, "Charisma" in *Dictionary of Biblical Languages with Semantic Domains: Greek (New Testament)* (Oak Harbor, WA: Logos Research Systems, Inc., 1997) 5922.
39. "Sbennymi," Strong's G4570, *Blue Letter Bible* online. Available at www.blueletterbible.org.
40. Sam Storms, "Seven Ways to Quench the Spirit," DesiringGod.org, April 29, 2018, https://www.desiringgod.org/articles/seven-ways-to-quench-the-spirit.
41. Sam Storms, *Understanding Spiritual Gifts* (Grand Rapids, MI: Zondervan, 2020), 178,189.
42. Priscilla Shirer, "Fire Fall Down," GoingBeyond.com, March 1, 2020, https://www.goingbeyond.com/jewelry-box/fire-fall-down/.
43. David Lang, "A "Do Not Be Afraid" for Every Day of the Year?", AccordanceBible.com, June 22, 2012, https://www.accordancebiblecom/a-do-not-be-afraid-for-every-day-of-the-year/.
44. O. Betz, "Might, Authority, Throne," ed. Lothar Coenen, Erich Beyreuther, and Hans Bietenhard, *New International Dictionary of New Testament Theology* (Grand Rapids, MI: Zondervan, 1986), 601.

Also from Jeannie Cunnion

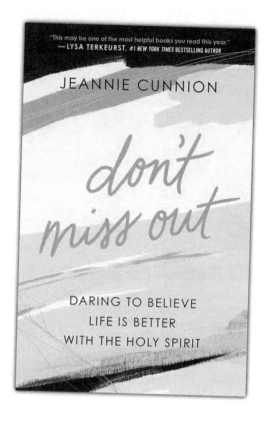

Though she had been following Jesus for more than thirty-five years as a pastor's kid, Jeannie Cunnion was surprised to realize that she was missing out on experiencing *all* of God. In this empowering invitation to discover the work of the Holy Spirit in you, she bids you to welcome the Spirit's guidance in your life and dive deeper into the transforming love of Jesus.

Don't Miss Out

Get the most from your study.

In this 7-session study by Jeannie Cunnion, discover how the Holy Spirit's presence and power transform how you lead and love your kids. You'll be invited to wrestle through the question, *Do I really know how to parent in the power of the Holy Spirit, or have I settled for parenting in my own power?*

In this study you'll:

- Come to know the Holy Spirit as your intimate Companion and Friend.
- Deepen your understanding of the Holy Spirit's role in your spiritual growth.
- Learn how to discuss the Holy Spirit with your children.
- Experience the freedom that comes from resting in the Holy Spirit, as you depend on Him to shepherd your children's hearts.

ADDITIONAL RESOURCES

Visit **lifeway.com/neveralone** to explore both the Bible study book and eBook along with a free sample session and church promotional materials.